When the Light Comes Quietly

Reflections on Loss, Healing, and the God Who Stays

Terasha Burrell

When The Light Comes Quietly: Reflections on Loss, Healing, and The God Who Stays
Printed in the United States of America.

All scripture quotations are taken from the Holy Bible, New International Version, New Living Translation, Amplified Bible, and The Christian Standard Bible.

For wholesale orders or inquiries contact:
terashaburrell@gmail.com

Disclaimer: This book is based on real experiences. To protect the privacy of others, some names and identifying details have been changed, and certain details have been blended or compressed.

ISBN- 979-8-218-85554-3

How to Read This Book

Hey friend, hey!

Thank you for being here. I know it takes courage to pick up a book about grief. The last thing I wanted to do in the thick of my own loss was read about it. Imagine how hard it is to write one while you're still living it.

This book won't ask you to have answers, peace, or steady faith. It won't rush you toward healing or hand you easy comfort. What it will do is walk with you—one person who's been in the dark to another who's still finding their way.

What You'll Find Here

This book holds two kinds of writing: personal reflections that read like essays (including the day I got mad as hell and threw every bowl I owned against the wall), and devotionals that weave Scripture, story, and gentle guidance together. There are also open pages throughout—space for your own words, memories, laments, and prayers.

I won't recount every loss or ask you to hold the full weight of my story. Instead, I'll share what I've been graced to share: the wrestling, the questions, the surprising ways God showed up when I thought He'd gone quiet.

How to Use It

There's no right way to move through these pages.

You can read one piece a day, giving yourself time to sit with each reflection and write when something stirs in you. Or you can read straight through, then return to the sections that tug at you later.

You can cry. You can laugh at my jokes (please laugh at my jokes). You can write in the margins or underline sentences that feel true. You can skip sections that feel too heavy right now and come back when you're ready.

However you move through it, my hope is that these pages make room for your story, your grief, and the quiet ways God is still with you.

A Gentle Warning

Your heart may be tender right now—too tender to sit with certain pieces of your story. This book touches on mental health, anger, and alcohol use. Some reflections may feel triggering or heavy. If you need to step away, take a breath, or return later, that's okay. Be kind to yourself as you read.

Dedication

For my Uncle Ken, you have lived through more loss than one heart should bear, but I am encouraged by how you keep knowing and trusting in the Lord.

And to my dad who loved us with everything he had: Your girls are alright. Your light lives on. And Roll Tide!

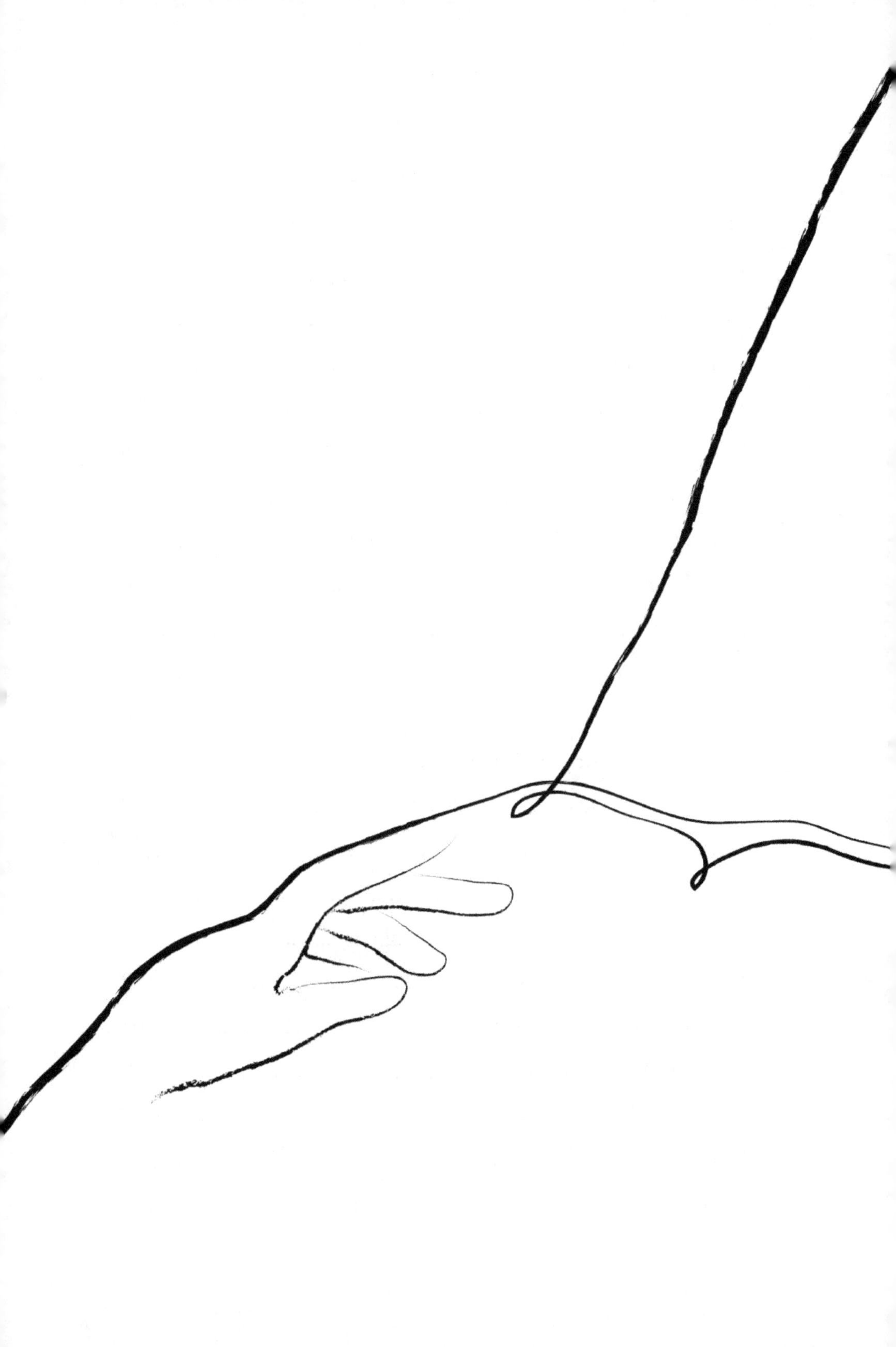

Contents

When The Light Went Out

Introduction

Every life holds a moment that quietly draws a line between before and after. When it comes, something in you changes for good. It is as if a light you depended on without ever noticing it has suddenly gone out.

My moment came June 11, 2024, at one o'clock in the morning.

The phone rang through the stillness of the night, the kind of ring that fills you with dread before you even answer. My father had died. After years of illness, his body finally surrendered. When I heard the words, "Your dad is gone," the world shifted. Everything felt both sharp and distant. The clock became the only sound. A metallic taste settled on my tongue. Even my own name felt unfamiliar.

A few days later, we planned his funeral for Father's Day. The timing felt poetically cruel and strangely fitting—honoring him and grieving him on the same day. I assumed this grief alone would undo me. I didn't know yet how much of my life would come apart in that same week.

We were in our new house, barely unpacked, boxes still lining the walls like we didn't quite believe we belonged there yet. The kitchen smelled faintly of cardboard and dust. I sat at the island, my hands wrapped around a mug I wasn't drinking from, staring at the granite.

He leaned against the back counter, arms folded, already somewhere else. The distance between us was small but deliberate, measured in inches and silence.

Three days after my father's funeral, less than two years into our marriage, I asked my husband, "Is there someone else?"

In the weeks that followed, I moved through my life like a stranger: making coffee, signing papers, sending polite texts, performing a version of normal while everything around me felt foreign. Grief blurred even the simplest tasks, as if I were living someone else's life.

One afternoon, I was in my new garden, trying to determine where to plant some begonias I'd purchased from the nursery. I was doing anything I could to keep myself busy. My father used to work as a landscaper in the summer months. When I was a teenager, I'd helped him with flower bed jobs, so without thinking, I reached for my phone and tapped his name in my call history to get some gardening advice.

When the recording said, "The number you have dialed is no longer in service," I froze. For a few moments, I just stood there, shaking my head, watering the soil with my tears.

Pretending I misdialed felt easier than facing the finality of silence.

The reality of everything I just walked through within a few weeks finally felt real. I tried to stay busy to outrun the ache, but grief does not let you escape—it waits for you to stop pretending.

Early grief felt like standing slightly outside myself. My mind, my body, even my faith felt off balance.

I tried to pray, but the words refused to come. Scripture blurred on the page. Verses I'd memorized since childhood suddenly felt like a foreign language. Worship felt hollow, like I was performing motions my body remembered but my heart couldn't access. I'd open my Bible to Psalms, those ancient laments that were supposed to meet me in the dark, and feel nothing. Just flatness. The worst part wasn't anger or confusion. Anger would have been something to feel. It was the terrifying silence, the sense that I was shouting into a void and nothing was shouting back. I wondered if God had dimmed with the lights, if maybe He only showed up in the good seasons, and now that everything had gone dark, He'd quietly slipped away too.

Learning how to navigate a world my dad no longer lived in felt like a Sims game where someone removed the instruction manual, deleted half the furniture, and expected me to keep playing like nothing had changed. Relearning how to do life as a single woman became its own puzzle. I could not escape my father's absence or the echo of broken promises. Both losses reshaped my understanding of life and love in ways I never expected.

Eventually, I stopped fighting and sat still. Some days, the stillness felt like punishment. Other days, it felt like a strange kind of peace. I sat with unanswered prayers, the empty chair across from me, and a home meant for two now holding only one.

Another afternoon, surrounded by half-unpacked boxes and curtains barely opened, something inside me gave way. I grabbed a stack of bowls and threw them against the wall. Not just one bowl. Every bowl I could reach. The crash was the first loud sound in the house in weeks, finally matching the chaos inside me.

Among the shattered pieces, one jagged shard caught my eye. I sat with it for a long time. The mess did not fix my life, but it told the truth. I felt shattered. Things had gotten dark. The darkness didn't rush in. It waited. It sat with me on the floor, among the broken pieces, and for the first time, I didn't try to outrun it.

Slowly, something began to shift. I was afraid of the dark, but it wasn't cruel. It was quiet. It stripped the noise away and forced me to sit still long enough to notice what I'd been missing. At first, I couldn't see anything at all. Then my eyes adjusted. Shapes appeared. Outlines returned.

I began to notice small mercies slipping in: a song that made me cry in the car, the smell of coffee in the morning, the sound of rain on the roof. These ordinary moments reminded me I was still cared for.

That is what this book is about: learning to live in the dark while you slowly begin to notice the quiet ways the light shows up.

When those small mercies began to return in my life, something in me softened toward the people who might be standing in their own dark rooms. I remembered how it felt to reach for hope and grab only air. How hard it was to breathe, pray, rest, or believe anything good could grow again.

So I wrote this book. It holds reflections from my own journey through compound loss and devotionals that will gently point you back to Scripture. Not to give you answers or rush you toward healing, but to walk alongside you. To remind you that God stays, even when everything else feels gone.

So if you are sitting in that kind of darkness now, I will not tell you to move on or hand you easy answers. Instead, pause right here with me.

Breathe in for four counts. Out for four counts. Do it again.

If you are grieving, there is a good chance you have not given yourself space to just breathe. Let your body remember what calm feels like. I will wait.

Picture us at a small table with two cups of coffee between us, or matcha if you prefer juiced grass. You do not have to explain anything. You do not have to pretend you are okay. You can stare at the floor. You can be silent. You can talk.

If I could reach across the table, I would tell you gently: You are not crazy for feeling everything and nothing at the same time. You are not faithless for being angry. You are not weak because prayer feels impossible. The ache in your chest, the exhaustion that will not lift, the sudden tears—none of it means you are broken beyond repair. It means you have loved deeply.

I do not have a map or a timeline to hand you. But I can walk with you. And I can promise this: God is still here, even if you cannot see Him yet.

So let's begin.

What If I Don't Know How to Swim?

A Reflection

People say grief comes in waves. They mean it as comfort, I think—a reminder that the intensity will ebb and flow, that you won't drown forever. But standing in the middle of it, you don't really need poetry about waves. You need someone to sit with you in the wreckage and not rush you toward the shore. Ok, I realize this is coming in a little hot (Terasha, please it's page seven). Honestly, when people say this to you while you're deep in grief, it feels like they're Rose on the shipwreck debris, telling you to hang on as you freeze, even though there's clearly enough space for both of you on that big piece of wood. I know that's dramatic. But that's what it felt like—people offering comfort while keeping themselves safe and separate. What I mean is: what I needed wasn't someone cheering from the shore. I needed someone willing to share it.

Okay, okay, okay. I don't *actually hate* the wave metaphor. It's a true sentiment about moving through grief. On good days, it helps. But in those early months, when someone would tell me about waves, I'd nod politely while thinking: "Sure, but which wave is this one? And how many more are coming? And can I just lie down on the beach instead?"

Because here's what the wave metaphor misses: you don't get a weather report for grief. There's no forecast or caution flags telling you to brace for impact on Tuesday afternoon, or that Thursday will be calm enough to get through a work meeting without falling apart. The waves just come. And sometimes they come from directions you didn't even know existed.

Every time someone says it, though, I think about a joke my dad used to make.

Any conversation about waves and water would set him off. Fishing, the beach, cruises, boats of any kind. My dad didn't know how to swim, but it never stopped him from going on any water adventure. He loved the water. At some point, he would work in one of his favorite jokes, one I'd heard a million times.

"But I can bet you if somebody threw me into the deep end, I'd learn to swim real quick."

He'd say it with a confidence that made no sense. Then he'd laugh and tell the joke again.

Lately, I keep thinking about what he was really saying. Not that he couldn't swim, but that he would figure it out.

My dad wasn't talking about learning how to swim. Whether he knew it or not, he was talking about survival. My dad's joke was about that desperate moment—when instinct kicks in and you do whatever it takes to stay breathing. That's survival. And survival matters. But it's not all you do or need.

This is where the way people talk about grief coming in waves stops working for me.

Grief didn't feel like being thrown into the deep end of a pool where I could eventually touch bottom, grab the edge, or rely on a lifeguard to scoop me up. It didn't feel like falling or being thrown overboard on a cruise ship, where someone would notice, sound an alarm, and pull me back in.

It felt like a shipwreck. Like Tom Hanks in *Cast Away*, stranded in the middle of an endless ocean, surrounded by debris. Not just driftwood or coconuts, but the remnants of a life that used to make sense—routines, plans, the future I thought we'd have, conversations I'd never get to finish. All of it bobbing just out of reach. The water was cold and unrelenting, tugging at me, filling every hollow space I didn't know I had. It pressed against my lungs, made my limbs heavy, and carried the silence of a world that had moved on without me.

And here's the thing about a shipwreck: if you don't already know how to swim or even any basics, you don't learn to swim at that moment. You just grab whatever's close, hold on, and pray for rescue.

My dad was right about one part. When you hit the water, you do learn something quick. But that's not the same as learning to swim. When thrown into grief and you have no idea what to do, you learn. You learn how to survive.

Survival didn't feel or look brave.

It looked like answering "I'm fine" because the truth required more words than I had.

It looked like staying so busy I didn't have time to feel the weight of the water pressing in on me.

Survival was necessary. But survival is just: don't drown right now. And that's not sustainable.

At some point, I realized I needed more than "right now." Because if I didn't know when, how big, or how long the waves would last, I needed something to orient me. I needed a way to stay afloat even when no one was coming. Something that said, you can rest here. You can breathe here. You don't have to master the ocean today.

That's when survival started to shift. Not into swimming, not yet, but into floating. Into trusting that staying above water counted as part of the process. Into believing that holding on was not weakness, but wisdom.

I can't tell you exactly when it happened. There wasn't a moment where everything clicked into place.

For me, it started with small things.

Therapy became something to hold onto—a place where I could name the weight I was carrying without apologizing for it.

A grief group became a life raft where I could finally stop treading water. It was full of people who understood that some days you do not share updates or breakthroughs. You just show up and cry, and that is the whole meeting.

Most importantly, honest prayers became the rope I held tightest when the waves came. Not the polished kind. The kind that sounded more like gasping than praise. The kind that simply said, "God, I do not know how to do this."

Some days, learning looked like getting through the day with the smallest possible goals. Brush my teeth. Drink water. Eat something with actual nutrients. Step outside for five minutes and let the sun hit my face, proof the world was still turning even when I felt stuck.

Some days, learning looked like letting someone bring dinner and not apologizing for needing it.

Some days, learning looked like answering one text instead of disappearing for a week.

Over time, the waves changed. Sometimes they were smaller. Sometimes they weren't. Sometimes I thought I was doing better and then a smell, a date, a holiday, or a random Tuesday wave knocked me clean off my feet.

The waves did what waves do. They showed up. They left. They showed up again.

I'm learning that the waves aren't trying to drown me. They're just moving. And maybe I can move with them. Maybe

I can hold onto what keeps me steady and let the water carry me without letting go.

I'm not doing grief wrong. I'm doing grief human. And that means I'm learning as I go—slowly, imperfectly, but still learning.

And somewhere in the middle of all this water, I can still hear my dad's voice. Not the joke about the deep end this time. Something quieter. Something that sounds like: You're still here. That means you're learning, baby girl.

And he's right. I am learning.

But I'm also starting to wonder if learning how to swim isn't actually the point. If surviving isn't either.

I spent so long trying to figure out how to do this on my own. Trying to learn the rhythms, grab the right wreckage, time the waves, keep my head above water. And all of that mattered. It kept me breathing.

But somewhere along the way, I started thinking that if I just held on tight enough, learned fast enough, got strong enough, I could make it to shore by myself.

And maybe that's not what this is about.

Maybe God isn't asking me to figure it out.

Maybe God is saying, "I'm coming for you."

There's this verse in Psalm 18 that keeps showing up for me: *He reached down from on high and took hold of me; he drew me out of deep waters.*

He reached down. He took hold. He drew me out.

I keep coming back to that. Because it doesn't say He taught me how to swim. It doesn't say He coached me from the shore or reminded me that waves come in sets or told me I was strong enough to do this on my own.

He reached down and pulled me out.

And I think that's what I'm learning to trust. That God doesn't stand on the shore calling instructions. God gets in the water.

God sits in the wreckage with me when I'm too tired to move. Rides the waves with me when they come. Parts the waves when I need to breathe. Carries me when my arms give out.

I'm still learning to trust that kind of rescue when you're still in the water, the waves keep coming, and you're used to doing everything on your own.

Some days, it looks like letting someone sit with me in the silence.

Some days, it looks like whispering a prayer I'm not even sure I believe yet, just because I need to say it out loud.

Some days, it looks like admitting I can't do this alone and trying to let that be okay.

Some days, it looks like resting—not because I've earned it, but because maybe God says rest is part of rescue too.

I don't know when the rescue will come. I just know I'm not meant to drown here. I don't know if it's a dramatic parting-of-the-Red-Sea moment or a slow, quiet gathering-up that happens so gently I don't even notice until I realize my feet are on solid ground again.

But here's what I'm learning: I'm not out here alone.

God is in the water with me. That's not theology I'm trying to prove—it's the thing that keeps me breathing when the waves come.

So maybe my dad's joke was closer to the truth than I thought, just not the way he meant it. He said he'd learn real quick if somebody threw him in the deep end. And I think if he were here, we'd laugh and I'd add: "Yeah, Dad. You'd figure out real quick that you need help."

Because that's what I'm learning.

Survival isn't the same as rescue.

Learning to swim isn't the same as being carried.

Holding on is good, but being held is better.

And maybe that's what faith looks like in the water. Not conquering the waves. Just waiting. Holding on. Trying to trust the One who's already here with me.

Some days, that's all the faith I've got.

But I'm starting to think that might be enough.

Still Close

A Verse to Hold

"The Lord is close to the brokenhearted and saves those who are crushed in spirit."

Psalm 34:18 (NIV)

Some verses wait for the moment they will matter. You can read them for years, nod along, highlight them in your Bible, and still not feel their weight until life knocks the wind out of you. Psalm 34:18 is one of those verses. It steps forward when grief shows up and suddenly resonates in a new way, almost like God saying, *I know this hurts. I am right here.*

Grief has a way of changing what you hear. It can turn the world you once knew into something unfamiliar. You may look at the same rooms, talk to the same people, follow the same routines, and still feel like a stranger in your own life. That is the thing about sorrow—it rearranges everything. It slows some things down and sharpens others. It can make you question what you believed and feel vulnerable in places you never noticed before.

This verse meets you right in the middle of that shift. It does not tell you to be strong or pull yourself together. It simply tells you where God chooses to stand. The Hebrew picture behind the word close is intimate. It means God leans in. He comes near enough to hear the cracking of your voice and the grief you do not say out loud. He is not waiting for you to hand Him a polished prayer. He is paying attention to the ache that sits in your chest.

The Lord is close to the brokenhearted. He saves those who are crushed in spirit.

Those words are honest about two things at once. First, brokenness is real. There is no pretending here. God does not downplay the weight of sorrow or ask you to ignore what hurts. Second, His presence inside that brokenness is real too. He does not stand at a distance. He does not wait for the pain to lighten. He steps into it with you.

Sometimes His work of deliverance is strong and obvious, like a breakthrough you never saw coming. But more often it is quiet. It looks like getting out of bed on a morning when you wanted to stay hidden. It looks like a moment of peace in a week of chaos. It looks like a strength you did not know you had until you needed it. His rescue does not always change your situation right away. Sometimes it changes you in the middle of it.

And somewhere in that slow work, a truth becomes clear: closeness is not something we have to earn. It is something He chooses to give simply because we are His.

Grief touches every part of who you are. It can reach into your identity, your sense of safety, your hopes for the future. It can make you wonder who you are now that life looks different. Yet God meets every version of grief with the same tenderness. He sits with the one who lost a loved one. He steadies the one whose relationship fell apart. He strengthens the one whose dream dissolved. He listens to the one who feels embarrassed by a decision they never wanted to make. There is no version of sorrow that makes Him pull back.

If you look back over your own story, you may notice moments that held you even when you felt like you were unraveling. After my father passed, there were nights when the silence in my house felt heavy, but something gentle kept me steady enough to move through each day. I did not have words for it then, but now I can see it for what it was. That was closeness. Not dramatic, not loud, just steady enough to carry me. The presence of God does not erase pain, but it transforms how it sits inside you. His nearness becomes the reminder that sorrow does not get the final say—He does. Hope may return in small pieces, but it returns. Strength may arrive little by little, but it arrives. Joy may come quietly at first, but it still comes.

Psalm 34:18 is not limited to one kind of heartbreak. It does not expire or narrow its reach. It is a promise wide enough for anyone who is trying to live with what they never wanted to lose. The Lord is close. And His closeness is enough.

In Prayer

God, meet me in the places that feel heavy and tender. I do not always have the right words, but You know the ache I am carrying. Draw close to the parts of me that feel broken and unsure. Give me strength for today and rest for the pieces of me that are tired. Remind me that I am not walking through this alone and that Your love stays even when everything else feels shaken. Be close to me, God, and let Your closeness be enough. Amen.

Sit with this

Where can you see signs of God's closeness in the midst of your losses?

What fears about the next season can you surrender to the God who promises to stay near?

Cry-Baby

A Verse to Hold

"You keep track of all my sorrows. You have collected all my tears in your bottle; You have recorded each one in your book."

Psalm 56:8 (NIV)

There is something tender about the image of collecting tears. In ancient times, mourners would catch their tears in small bottles called lachrymatory vessels and place them in tombs as evidence of their grief. The tears were proof that someone was loved, that someone was missed. Psalm 56:8 tells us that God does something similar, but infinitely more personal: He collects our tears in His bottle. The imagery is so vivid, so personal, that David felt compelled to write it. God does not watch our suffering from a distance. He is close enough to catch every tear. It is one of those verses you do not just read. You feel it.

God does not stay far away while we cry. He bends low. He pays attention. Nothing we have grieved has gone unnoticed. In a world that tells us to toughen up or move on, God says, "I saw that tear. I kept it."

We cry from places we cannot always explain. We cry from heartbreak, disappointment, confusion, loneliness, love. And while the world may rush past our sorrow, heaven does not. God gathers what falls from our eyes like something precious, something worth holding. Not to display our pain, but to show us that He never leaves us alone in it.

I learned this in a moment I will never forget. In the thick of my grief, when I was barely holding myself together, someone said to me: "You're not the first person to go through this, and you won't be the last." The words landed like a dismissal. I know they were likely meant to comfort, to remind me I was not alone. But what I heard was: your pain is common, unremarkable, nothing special. I held back what I wanted to say. I nodded. I walked away. And then I broke down in silence.

Because grief does not feel common when it is yours. It feels isolating and enormous and unbearably personal. It does not matter how many people have walked this road before—when you are the one walking it, it is the only road you can see.

That is what makes Psalm 56:8 so powerful. It does not minimize or compare. It does not tell you that your sorrow is just like everyone else's, so you should be fine by now. Instead, it says: God keeps track. He collects. He records each one. Your tears are not lost in a sea of everyone else's. They are yours, and He knows them.

Grief can make you feel invisible. You can be surrounded by people and still feel unseen. But this verse reminds us that God notices the moments no one else catches. The tears cried in the car. The ones shed quietly at night. The ones you wipe quickly so you do not have to explain. He sees the full weight of what we carry, even when we carry it in silence.

This promise does not mean the pain disappears. It means the pain is witnessed. The nights you could not pray because the sorrow was too deep were still heard. He saw the questions that never formed into words, the ache that felt too heavy to name. He holds every moment, not for judgment, but for redemption.

The psalms are full of this kind of honesty—raw prayers from people who knew what it felt like to be overwhelmed. David wrote from caves and battlefields, from seasons of victory and seasons of loss. He knew what it was to feel forgotten, to wonder if God was listening. And yet he also knew this: God does not turn away from tears. He moves toward them.

When we grieve, we often encounter people who mean well but say things that sting. They tell us it could be worse. They remind us that time heals all wounds. They assure us that everything happens for a reason. And sometimes, like me, we have to smile and nod and hold back what we really want to say. We have to carry both the original grief and the new wound of being misunderstood.

But God does not require us to explain ourselves. He does not ask us to make sense of our sorrow before coming near or compare our pain to someone else's. He simply stays. He watches. He records. And in doing so, He dignifies what we feel. Our tears matter because we matter. Not as one of many, but as His beloved.

He does not waste what we have wept over. In His hands, even our sorrow is treated like seed, planted with care for a harvest we cannot yet see. As the psalmist wrote, "Those who sow in tears will reap with songs of joy" (Psalm 126:5). This is not a promise that grief will be brief or that pain will resolve quickly. It is a promise that what we plant in tears, the faithfulness we offer even when it hurts, the trust we extend without understanding, will not return void.

Sometimes we imagine God most present in the miracles, in the celebrations, in the answered prayers that make everything bright again. But Psalm 56:8 reveals a tender truth often overlooked: God is intimately present in the dim rooms where our tears fall. He does not wait for us to be healed before He draws near. He meets us in the breaking.

There is a difference between a God who observes and a God who collects. One watches from a safe distance. The other bends close enough to catch what falls. The God of

Scripture is the latter. He is the God who knelt in the Garden of Gethsemane and wept. The God who stood at Lazarus's tomb and let His tears fall with Mary's and Martha's. The God who understands what it is to grieve, not as an idea, but as an experience.

If your heart feels heavy today, you can rest in this. God is not asking you to be strong or to pull yourself together. He is near when your hands shake and when you feel forgotten. He is near the parts of your story you do not want but cannot change. You do not have to fix what is broken before He will show up. He is already there, holding what you cannot carry alone.

And one day, when healing has done its slow and holy work, you will see that none of your sorrow was wasted. The tears you cried were not lost. They were kept. They were known. They were held by a God who loves you more tenderly than you can imagine.

They were not the end of your story. They were the seeds of what God would one day redeem.

In Prayer

Father, thank You for being near to the brokenhearted and for keeping track of every tear I've ever cried. Remind me that nothing has been lost on You, not one ache, not one question, not one cry in the dark. Teach me to see my tears as seeds You have planted for something redemptive and beautiful. Help me to believe that even when I do not understand, You are still working for my good. May my tears become testimony, my sorrow become strength, and my grief become the ground where Your grace grows something new. Amen.

Sit with this

Think about the seasons in your life that have brought the most tears. Which moments do you still feel God inviting you to hand over to Him?

What might it mean to trust that those tears were not wasted, but planted?

Write down one specific sorrow that you want to believe has purpose, even if you cannot yet see the harvest it will bring.

When God Doesn't Do What You Hoped

A Verse to Hold

"As the heavens are higher than the earth, so are my ways higher than your ways and my thoughts than your thoughts."

Isaiah 55:9 (NIV)

I knew this verse long before grief touched my life, but I did not fully understand it until disappointment came and sat heavy on my chest. I thought I trusted God's ways, but I expected those ways to look like the outcomes I prayed for. I expected healing, restoration, a miracle. I never expected a chapter that felt so far from anything I asked Him for.

Isaiah 55:9 tells us plainly that God sees what we cannot. His ways stretch higher than our longing, wider than our understanding, and deeper than our expectations. I believed that in theory. I just did not expect to learn it through heartbreak.

There is one night I return to whenever I read this verse. It was a few weeks after my dad passed. I pulled into the driveway, turned off the car, and just sat there. I did not want to walk into a house that felt too quiet. I did not want to face the reality that life had gone in a direction I never prayed for.

The dashboard lights were the only glow in the car. I scrolled my phone, skipped songs, blinked back tears, and tried to avoid the truth sitting in my chest. Eventually I let out a long breath and prayed the most honest sentence I had ever prayed: *This is not what I asked You for.*

That is where Isaiah 55:9 meets real life.

When God's ways feel nothing like the ways we hoped for. When His thoughts do not line up with our plans. When His version of healing does not look anything like ours.

Disappointment can make you feel like you misunderstood God. It can make you question everything you thought you knew. You pray, fast, believe, and still end up holding a story you never wanted. It becomes the filter you see life through. It raises questions you never imagined asking: *Can I trust You with what hurts this much? Can I believe You are good when the outcome feels cruel?*

But here is where the verse begins to soften the ache. God is not threatened by our disappointment. He is not offended by our honesty. He knows the distance between heaven and earth. He knows how limited our view is, how much we long for outcomes that feel gentle. And He also knows what we cannot see.

As the weeks passed, I learned that surrender is not pretending you trust God. Surrender is trusting that His higher ways sometimes pass straight through valleys we never would have chosen. Some days I trusted easily. Other days I snatched back my trust like Rashad snatching New New's necklace in the movie ATL. And even in that, God stayed patient.

I had to face something I still wrestle with: my prayers were shaped by longing. God's answer was shaped by eternity.

I wanted one more day, one more breath, one more chance. But now my dad experiences the wholeness and healing that only eternity with God provides—free from all pain and limitation. And painful as it was, the love between us did not end the day he left. It simply changed form, a bond that death cannot sever.

Isaiah 55:9 also reminds us that if it were up to us, we would write stories without endings. No loss. No separation. No goodbyes. But we do not write these stories. We live inside them, right in the tension between what is beautiful and what is broken. And in that tension, God stays close.

He stays when the questions are loud. He stays when disappointment weighs more than hope. He stays when His ways confuse us or stretch us or break us open.

That is why disappointment is not the end of faith. It is often the beginning, where faith shifts from trusting outcomes to trusting presence. In that space, Isaiah 55:9 becomes more than a verse. It becomes a lifeline.

Looking back, I can say this with a steadier heart. God was walking with me through a story I never chose, not to harm me but to hold me. He was guiding me through a chapter where, despite the pain, He would meet me and teach me to trust Him in new ways—not just with the miracles I prayed for, but with the mourning I never expected.

The story did not end the way I pictured. But even in the disappointment, God is still writing something beautiful. And His ways, always higher, have never lost sight of me.

In Prayer

Father, I bring You my disappointment, the prayers that went unanswered, the healing I longed to see, the miracle that never came. Teach me to trust You here. Fill me with Your thoughts when mine feel heavy. Help me to see that even in loss, You are still working. Remind me that Your love remains higher than my understanding, and Your presence is still near to the brokenhearted. Amen.

Sit with this

What disappointment in your grief still feels hard to talk to God about?

How might surrendering your expectations open space for God to comfort you in new ways?

I'm Mad as Hell

A Reflection

I honestly didn't know how I expected anger to look in grief. I knew the stages, and people were kind enough to remind me that they come without warning and out of order. Sadness felt predictable. Shock, sure. Numbness, absolutely. But anger? That one felt like a stranger. I assumed anger would storm in, throw things around, make a scene. And it did. But I didn't expect the quieter parts of anger, the kind that sits in your body like a stone because something you love has been ripped away. When it finally rose in me, it startled me. I didn't know anger could feel this tender or this raw.

What made it harder was the guilt that followed. I knew how to cry. I knew how to pray. No one ever taught me what to do when grief lit a fire in my chest. I grew up thinking anger meant I had stepped outside of faith somehow. That if I were really trusting God, I wouldn't feel this way. But the anger came anyway. It came honest and steady, and I had to face the truth. It wasn't a failure. It wasn't rebellion. It was the part of me still trying to breathe through what felt impossible.

One afternoon, a few days after my dad passed, I was sitting on the back patio of my parents' house with my mom.

The patio had become their place after 40 years of marriage, and their backyard felt like a slow exhale. My father had designed and built the landscaping with his own hands, and you could feel him in everything. We sat in their favorite lawn chairs staring out at the overgrown vegetable garden that was my dad's pride and joy. It was the sweetest thing to watch them in the garden together picking cucumbers, tomatoes, squash, and watermelon. It was also the source of many jokes as my dad fussed at us if we picked one thing wrong or stepped where we shouldn't. The back patio was where they would spend every evening the temperature allowed. It was where we gathered as a family daily after he was gone.

This day was just me and her. Not many words between us. We just sat leaned back in their chairs enjoying the breeze and the singing of the windchimes that peeked out from various spots of the landscaping.

The relationship my mother and I have is sweet. She and I are honest with each other, even though she still reminds me that she is not one of my little friends. We were super quiet for a while and then I said, "Mama, I am mad as hell that dad died." I let the windchimes cover the crack in my voice. "I am mad at him, and I don't know why."

She nodded gently and said, "Me too."

That moment felt so sacred. Holy even. Two people acknowledging that love can make you angry when its story ends too soon.

Telling my mom was one thing. Telling God felt like another thing entirely.

The anger I feared most was the anger I carried toward God. I could not understand why the miracle I prayed for did not come. The timing felt harsh. If this was His will, it felt unkind. I found myself asking questions I never thought I would ask.

God, do you even care about what I long for?

Did you ever have plans to heal him?

When I looked at Scripture, though, I realized I was not the only one. David questioned God in the middle of his fear. Jeremiah cried out from the depths of his sorrow. Job demanded answers that made everyone around him uncomfortable. Even Jesus asked for the cup to pass from him. If blood, sweat, and tears isn't a form of holy anger, I don't know what is. Seeing these stories lined up beside my own made me feel less alone. They reminded me that God has always welcomed honesty, even the kind that shakes in your hands.

But God wasn't the only target. I also felt anger toward people around me. Friends who grew distant. People who tried to comfort me but missed the mark. Watching life move forward for others while mine felt like it was slipping out from under me made something inside me tighten. Not because I wished anyone harm, but because everything felt unfair. Grief has a way of showing you that the world will not sit with you in your pain.

Layered on top of that was the pressure of being the strong one. People kept telling me how well I was carrying everything, how I didn't look like what I had been through. They meant it as affirmation, but it created a kind of confinement. As a Black woman, I already knew anger was a stereotype waiting for me the moment I let my guard down. I didn't want to be seen as the angry Black woman. I didn't want to be the perfectly strong one either. Both roles kept people from checking on me, so I often sat alone on this journey.

My anger turned inward quickly. I replayed my marriage like a movie I couldn't shut off. I kept wondering if I should have noticed something sooner, or fought harder, or been someone different. And then came the anger I didn't expect. I was mad at myself for leaving, even though staying would have broken me in a different way. I was mad that I couldn't seem to get this part of my life right, like everyone else had received a manual I somehow missed. Divorce made me feel like I had failed at something I was supposed to know how to hold, even though the truth was far more complicated. I took on blame that didn't belong to me and carried shame for a weight that was never mine to carry alone. Little by little, I learned that anger at myself was just another part of grief, not a verdict on my worth.

Then came the anger I never saw coming. The anger at myself over my dad dying. I didn't even know you could be angry at yourself for a death you did not cause. But I replayed phone calls. I questioned whether I should have visited more. I wondered if I should have prayed harder or paid closer attention to things none of us could control. That kind of anger is irrational, but grief does not always follow reason. It exposes every corner where you believe you could have done better. It becomes its own courtroom, and you become both judge and defendant.

And then there were days when I even felt anger toward my dad. Not in blame, but in the ache of being left behind. I didn't expect love and anger to sit in the same space inside me, but they did. That is part of grief too.

Anger protected me at first. It worked like a shield, helping me stand when everything felt unsteady. But it didn't stay protective for long. Slowly, it turned into a weight, building walls that kept more in than they kept out. I felt it in my body. My shoulders stayed tight. My sleep shifted. My reactions came quicker than I could explain. My mind stayed on alert, trying to grab control of a world that refused to behave. I started to realize that anger often speaks for fear before fear can find the words.

And that's when the bowl-smashing incident happened. It was every bit as dramatic as the movies.

The boxes had been sitting there for months. Brown cardboard towers with my hasty Sharpie labels: "Kitchen" and "Guest room closet" and one that just said "Misc" because by the end of the move I'd stopped caring what went where. They lined the hallway of my new home like unpaid debts, items wrapped in packing paper and towels because I'd run out of proper packing paper and patience on the same day.

The walls around them were bare. Not minimalist-bare. Paralysis-bare. The kind of empty that happens when you move into a place that's supposed to be a fresh start but you can't make yourself hang a single picture because that would mean admitting you live here now. That this is real.

I'd been stepping around these boxes for so long I'd worn a path in the carpet. Living out of them like a squatter in my own home. Using one plate, one fork, one towel, because actually unpacking meant actually moving forward, and I wasn't ready for that.

But that Tuesday (I don't even remember what day of the week it actually was, but it feels like it should have been a Tuesday) something shifted. Maybe I was tired of eating cereal standing at the counter. Maybe I'd finally run out of clean clothes and remembered there were more in one of those boxes. Maybe I just woke up and decided that this, at least, was a problem I could solve.

I started with the box labeled "Kitchen."

The tape screamed as I pulled it back. Inside: my everyday plates, still wrapped from a kitchen I'd cooked in with someone else. A wooden board that had been a wedding present that now felt like it belonged to a different person's life. Dishtowels I didn't remember packing. And there, nested together and wrapped in packing paper was a stack of glass cereal bowls.

I don't know what happened. One moment I was unwrapping them, and the next I was standing in the middle of my empty kitchen with this stack of bowls raised above my head like some kind of warrior, except I wasn't fighting anything that could be defeated by broken glass.

I threw them.

The sound they made when they hit. God, it was everything I wanted it to be. Not one crash but a cascade of them, each bowl shattering into the next. Sharp. Final. Satisfying in a way nothing else had been for months. The explosion of glass across the hardwood felt like punctuation at the end of a sentence I'd been trying to finish since everything fell apart.

And then: silence. My breath ragged. My arms still above my head. Four (or was it five?) bowls in a thousand pieces, and me standing in the middle of it like an idiot in a home I still couldn't call home.

Because here's what the movies don't show you: the moment after. When you realize that smashing something doesn't actually fix anything. When you look at what you've done and understand that all you've accomplished is creating another problem that needs solving. When you have to go find the broom (still in its box somewhere, probably) and start sweeping up the evidence of your small, useless rebellion.

I found a piece of one of those bowls under the couch three weeks later. Another shard embedded itself in my sock four months after that. To this day, I'll be walking across the kitchen and feel that familiar tiny bite against my heel, and I'll think: still here. Still not clean. Still finding pieces of the thing I thought I could shatter my way through.

I'm convinced they're multiplying just to keep me humble.

Breaking things had felt powerful in the moment, but it didn't actually empty me of anything. The mess was still there. The grief was still there. The anger was still there. And eventually, I ran out of things to throw and places to hide from it. I sat on the floor of that kitchen, surrounded by glass I'd have to sweep up eventually, and realized I had nowhere left to put this anger. I had thrown it at bowls. I had carried it in my body. I had avoided it in boxes. And it was still there. So I did the only thing I had left, what I should have done first. I brought it to God.

When I finally brought my anger to God in its full form, something shifted. I didn't bring a polished prayer or a calm voice. I brought the whole jumble of it, the frustration, the questions, the parts of myself I thought were too messy to name out loud. And He did not correct me or pull away. He didn't ask me to settle or calm down. He did not condescendingly say relax. He stayed with me.

In that quiet, I learned something I wish I had known earlier. The emotions I feared would separate me from God were the ones that actually drew Him closer. I expected judgment or disappointment, but neither came. Instead, I felt the steady presence of Someone who already knew the truth and was not intimidated by it. He was not threatened by my anger. He was not put off by my honesty. He was simply near.

So what do I do with my anger now?

Spiritually, I take it to God. Not the polished version, the real one. The "I am mad, and I do not understand" prayers. I have learned He can handle my honesty better than I can handle pretending.

Some days that honesty sounds like a whisper. Other days it sounds like, "Lord, you saw that, right?" I used to think I had to soften the edges before I came to God, like I needed to show up with a lesson already learned. Grief is giving me a new perspective of that. Now I come with the questions that have teeth, the ones that keep me up at night, the ones that do not fit on a pretty coffee mug.

I bring Him the parts of my anger that feel unfair. I tell Him when I am tired of being the strong one, when I am jealous of people who did not get this kind of loss, and when I do not like the way this story is unfolding. I do not always get reasons, but I do get reassurance that He is near. I get a God who sits in it with me instead of backing away.

So when I say I take my anger to God, I do not mean I tie it up with a bow. I mean I walk in with it still hot, still loud, still confused, and trust that He is big enough to hold what I am feeling and still call me His.

Practically, I had to find somewhere for all that fire to go because I couldn't keep breaking my own things. For me, that means the gun range. It is a controlled space where I can let some of that anger move through my body instead of into another broken dish or busting the windows out of someone's car. I put on the gear, focus, breathe, and for an hour my anger has somewhere safe to go. It gets me out of the house, around people, and my bowls live to see another day. I'm thinking about trying one of those rage rooms next—at least they don't make you sweep up after. The point is that my anger needs a safe outlet that does not harm me or make me an episode of Snapped. I would never say my way is for everyone. I am just learning what helps me tell the truth about how I feel without burning my whole life (or house) down.

For a long time, I carried guilt for being angry. I tried to keep it contained, to make it smaller, to act like it said something terrible about me. I hid it so no one would see it or ask questions I couldn't answer. But my anger would not disappear. It kept showing up because it was doing its job. It was signaling that something precious had been taken, and that deep loss had broken something inside me that could not be put back the same way.

What I do with that anger is where the choice lives now. That is where I keep asking God to meet me, to help me turn all that heat into something honest and healing, instead of something that burns me up from the inside.

I also learned that anger is not the opposite of faith. It can be part of faith. True faith is honest. True faith brings trembling words to God, not polished ones. Scripture reminds me that He is patient and rich in love. He never walked away from me in my wrestling. That is what His love looks like.

I don't have to be composed to be held by Him. I don't have to soften my anger or hide my trembling. Peace comes when I release what is too heavy for me to the One strong enough to carry it.

As grief continues to change me and anger weaves its way in and out of the story, I'm learning that none of it disqualifies me from healing or God's closeness. Not the questions, not the fear, not the days when my emotions feel louder than my faith. I can bring every feeling to God and still be held. I can be honest and still be comforted. I can be frustrated and still be guided toward peace. Healing is not something I earn by being composed. It's something He offers right in the middle of my mess and broken bowls.

The quiet miracle of anger in grief is this: healing did not come from hiding my anger. It came from bringing every part of it to God. Trusting that He would sit with me until the weight shifted, not quickly or dramatically, but slowly and gently, like breath returning after a long stretch of holding it.

And when anger finally loosened its grip, it felt like a breath I didn't know I had been waiting on. A small soft space opened inside me. A reminder that I am still here. A reminder that God is still here too. A reminder that even my anger could carry me toward healing in ways only He could understand.

Let Anger Speak

Take a quiet moment and pay attention to your body.

Where has anger been living lately:

Your jaw.

Your shoulders.

Your breath.

Your sleep.

Your reactions.

Let yourself name it without judging it. You are not weak for feeling it. You are human.

Think back to the moment your anger first appeared.

What were you afraid of losing?

What felt unfair?

Where did disappointment settle in your story?

Anger often points to the places where love has been stretched thin by pain.

Ask yourself gently:

What is my anger trying to protect?

What truth is it holding for me?

What ache have I not been able to admit out loud?

Now consider this: You do not have to carry anger alone. What would it look like to bring it to God without editing it. Without softening it. Without offering an explanation. Just honesty. Just your heart as it is.

Let yourself imagine Him sitting beside you. Not correcting you. Not rushing you. Just here. Steady, patient, and present.

Ask yourself:

If anger is a signal, what is it pointing to in me?

If anger is love with nowhere to go, where does that love still need tending?

If anger is not a failure, what permission do I need to give myself today?

Take a deep breath.

Offer God one sentence. It does not have to be pretty. It only needs to be true.

Then sit for a moment longer and notice any small place inside you that feels lighter. Not fixed.

Just open.

The work of healing often begins with the courage to be honest. Let today be a step toward that courage.

I Wasn't Ready for This

A Verse to Hold

"There is a time for everything, and a season for every activity under the heavens."

Ecclesiastes 3:1 (NIV)

There are moments in life that come without warning. Moments you did not plan for, did not agree to, and never felt ready to face. Losing a parent is one of them. The sentence that rises first is almost always the same: *I was not ready for this.* It is honest. It is raw. And it is true. No matter how old you are, there is no version of life where you feel prepared to lose someone who shaped your world.

Ecclesiastes says there is a time for everything, but what it does not say is that you will recognize the time when it comes. You do not get an alert before sorrow arrives. You do not get a countdown before life turns. Seasons shift quietly, and suddenly you are living in one you never would have chosen for yourself.

We love the verses about dancing, laughing, planting, and building. But Scripture places those right next to the verses about weeping, mourning, uprooting, and letting go. Not because we enjoy those seasons, but because they are also a part of God's design. Sooner or later, every life encounters a moment that was never on the calendar.

And when it comes, our first instinct is often control. We scramble for answers, structure, anything that might make the ground feel steady again. We want timelines for healing, deadlines for pain, clarity about what comes next. But grief does not follow our schedule. And God, in His mercy, does not hurry us through what requires time to heal.

Surrendering to God's timing is not passive. It is one of the hardest acts of faith. It is admitting, *Lord, I was not ready for this, but You knew this season would come. And You will meet me in it.* It means giving up the idea that if you had been more prepared, prayed differently, or planned better, this moment would have turned out another way. Readiness was never the requirement. Dependence is.

There is a kind of strength that shows up when you stop trying to skip the season you are in. When you take a shaky breath and say, *I do not like this, I do not understand this, but I will stay present to it because You are here.* That surrender is not resignation. It is trust—believing that God holds time even when time feels unkind to you.

Some days, surrender looks like getting out of bed. Other days, it looks like letting yourself cry without rushing to fix it. Sometimes it is choosing rest over productivity, or saying no, or whispering, *God, help me make it through this hour.* Seasons like these are not measured in accomplishments. They are measured in breaths.

You do not have to celebrate a season you did not choose or be grateful for the timing. But you can trust that God is present inside it, guiding you with a tenderness that does not rush or pressure. Ecclesiastes invites us to accept what we cannot change, not because the season is good, but because the God who holds it is.

And slowly, without asking your permission, healing begins to come. Not because you forced it, but because God faithfully carried you through. You start to see glimpses of life you did not think you would feel again. A meal tastes good. The sun feels warm. A memory brings a smile instead of a collapse. These moments are not signs of forgetting. They are signs that God is walking you through a season you never wanted but were never asked to face alone.

Every season under heaven is held by the same steady hands. Even this one. Even the one you were not ready for.

In Prayer

God, help me to recognize the season I'm in and to trust You in it. When I am tempted to rush or rebuild too soon, teach me to rest in the rhythm You have set. Remind me that the same hands that hold the beauty of spring also hold the stillness of winter. I surrender my timeline and my understanding to You. Let discernment take root in me, and let peace come from knowing that You make everything beautiful in its time. Amen.

Sit with this

What season am I in right now, and have I been trying to control it instead of allowing it to run its course?

What might God be asking me to tend, release, or rest from in this season so that He can do His deeper work in me?

Why Not Me?

A Verse to Hold

"I remain confident of this: I will see the goodness of the Lord in the land of the living. Wait for the Lord; be strong and take heart and wait for the Lord."

Psalm 27:13-14 (NIV)

There is a quiet grief that comes with waiting. It is not loud, but it lingers. You see others receive what you have been praying for: marriage, healing, children, purpose, peace. Something stirs deep inside. You are happy for them, but a quiet sadness follows you home. It is the kind that makes you whisper, *Lord, why not me?* Waiting can feel heavy. Prayers start to sound the same. Dreams fade, and hope wavers. You may wonder if God has forgotten your name. Yet even here, in the stillness, His goodness remains.

David knew that feeling too. When he wrote Psalm 27, he was hiding and uncertain about what the future would bring. He had seen God's faithfulness before, but the waiting was long. Still, he spoke to his own soul and said, *"I remain confident that I will see the goodness of the Lord."* That kind of faith does not come from having all the answers. It comes from trusting that

God's presence is still good, even when the outcome is not what you hoped for.

Perhaps waiting is not wasted time but sacred space. A space where your faith grows roots, where you learn to depend on peace that does not come from progress, and where you begin to trust God's heart more than His hand. Waiting can feel small, like your prayers are hitting the ceiling. But small does not mean overlooked. You are not forgotten. Waiting does not mean God has said no—it may mean not yet, and His timing is trustworthy.

The same God who paints the sunrise is faithful with the timing of your life, even when you cannot see His plan. If you are waiting for healing, He promises strength to carry you through. If you are waiting for provision, He promises to meet your needs. If you are waiting for love, He reminds you that you are already deeply loved. His character does not waver when life feels uncertain.

Sometimes the miracle is not in the answered prayer but in the heart that keeps believing. The lesson in waiting is learning to notice God's presence in what is while trusting Him with what will be.

I have seen God answer prayers in my life. I always longed for marriage, for partnership, for someone to share life with. When I finally held those desires in my hands, I felt that God had heard me. He did. But the covenant was broken, and now

I find myself living in the aftermath, learning how to carry what remains of that chapter and waiting again, this time for God to show me what comes next. After everything was finalized, my first instinct was to run. I wanted to rebuild somewhere new, to start fresh in a different place. Yet here I am, still in the home that once held our plans, waiting for God to give me the green light on His.

Some days, waiting hurts deeply because it is not the story any of us hoped for. But even in the ache, something begins to grow. Waiting teaches that hope can survive heartbreak and that peace can sit right beside pain. In this in-between place, we learn that God is working even here. He sustains, He provides, and He reminds us that His care is enough in seasons that make no sense. Like David, we can choose to believe that we will still see the goodness of the Lord.

That confidence is not passive. It is brave. It is the kind of hope that keeps whispering through tears, *God, You did not forsake me. I know You never will.*

In this tender season, let your heart rest in that truth. It is okay to feel both heartbreak and hope. Grieve what has not happened yet and still believe something good will. God has not stopped working. He is just not finished yet. One day, you will look back and see His fingerprints of grace throughout the waiting, even when you could not feel them.

In Prayer

Father, I know You see the desires of my heart. Some days it's hard to understand Your timing, but I trust that You are still good. When the wait is heavy, help me to lean into You. Teach me to sing even in the valley, to praise You in the day and through the night, believing that nothing is wasted in Your hands. Strengthen me to celebrate others without losing hope in Your plan for me. Amen.

Sit with this

What am I waiting for right now, and how has that shaped my definition of what "good" means in God's eyes?

In this season of waiting, where do I see God's character still present even if my circumstances don't feel "good"?

Have you Considered Job's Wife?

A Reflection

If you do not know me well, you might not guess that the stories in Scripture that linger with me the longest are the ones about women people tend to misunderstand. My people are the woman at the well, the woman caught in adultery, the woman with the issue of blood, and all the unnamed ones tucked in the shadows. We only see them in snapshots, but those moments show where their lives collided with Jesus. I think I love them because I have been those women in one way or another, or I have loved them, or I have sat beside them in different seasons of their life. And quietly among them lives Job's wife.

We are not told her name or her story or how she prayed. All we get is one sentence. One raw line that has made generations shake their heads. She asked her husband why he didn't curse God and die. Most people leap straight to judgment. But every time I hear her words, something different echoes in me. I hear a woman who had lost her entire world. A woman who buried her children. A woman whose body no longer had room to hold what life had handed her. Her words do not sound rebellious to me. They sound like someone whose soul finally cracked under the weight of grief.

When I read her story through the lens of my own grief, I don't see a cautionary tale. I see a mirror. She lost everything Job lost—stood in the same ashes, faced the same devastation, watched her husband's body break while her own heart had already shattered. When she finally spoke, her pain spoke with her. Her words weren't polished. They weren't careful. They were simply what honesty sounds like when life has taken too much. I don't hear weak faith. I hear a woman whose pain had grown louder than her prayers.

I understand her more than I used to. Grief rewrote the way I spoke too. It made me say things my spirit didn't mean, even though my pain did. It made me question what I once trusted without hesitation.

I learned that at my kitchen table a few months after separating from my husband. I remember staring at a cup of coffee I couldn't bring myself to drink. The steam had already disappeared, but I kept my hands wrapped around the mug anyway, like if I let go of it I might fall apart completely. The house was quiet in a way that didn't feel peaceful. It felt hollow, almost echoing, like the walls were listening while I tried to hold myself together.

I had been sitting there long enough to watch the sunlight shift across the floor, but I couldn't bring my mind to move with it. Every prayer I tried to shape felt too tidy for what was happening inside me. I kept reaching for the kind of prayer I'd been raised to believe was acceptable, but anything gentle or poetic got stuck somewhere behind my ribs.

What finally came out wasn't dressed up at all.

"God, you are cruel."

I whispered it like someone might overhear me even though I was completely alone. And once that crack opened, everything else followed. I told Him He had allowed too much cruelty in my life. That I hated it. That I had longed for this marriage for years, prayed over it, cried for it, and could not believe this was what it became.

And the strange thing was, I knew in my bones that God didn't cause the breakdown. I knew this wasn't His doing. But I was caught in that uncomfortable space of trying to make sense of what God allows and the free will of people who choose harm. I didn't have the theology for that kind of ache. My head couldn't stretch far enough to explain it, and my heart couldn't shrink small enough to ignore it.

I told Him I didn't know how to do this with Him right now, not without feeling angry with Him for letting it unravel the way it did.

A small part of me wondered if I had crossed a line, if those words made me unfaithful or ungrateful or whatever word church folks like to use when someone admits their heart is breaking in real time. But the truth was simple. Those words were all I had. They had been sitting in my chest for months, heavy and unspoken, and that morning at the table was the first time they finally rose to the surface.

If anyone had walked in at that moment, they probably would have called me foolish too. They might have assumed my faith was collapsing. But I don't think that's what was happening. That morning, I wasn't trying to curse God. I wasn't trying to walk away from Him. I was trying to survive what hurt. I was learning, without knowing it yet, that honesty sometimes sounds like breaking. And that breaking can still be brought to God.

What moves me most is what Scripture leaves unsaid. God does not silence Job's wife. He does not correct her. He does not remove her from the story. He lets her be human. She stays right there, honest and exhausted, still seen.

Somehow that reality has become a lifeline for me. God has never edited me out for being human.

There have been days in this journey when prayer felt too heavy to hold. Days when silence felt safer than speaking. Days when I confessed my truth to a friend because saying it to God felt too bold. And there have been days I opened my journal and the only words that came out were the ones I was taught to keep far away from holy things. Grief isn't polite. My prayers weren't either. I have pages of anger, pages of questions, and pages covered in curse words because I didn't have gentle language for the pain I was living. For a long time, I thought all of that made me unfaithful. It didn't. These pages are honest. They are part of my journey too.

When I look back now, I can see that God was not shocked by any of it. He never needed me to tidy myself up before coming to Him. He wasn't waiting for better language or cleaner emotions. He was after my heart, even the messy parts. Even the frustrated scribbles. Even the mornings when a sigh was all I could manage. God can handle my honesty. He has never been after my performance, only my pursuit of Him.

Seeing Job's wife through this lens doesn't make me want to cling to bitterness. It simply gives me permission to acknowledge how grief behaves in me. Sometimes pain speaks before hope does. Sometimes questions rise before my faith steadies. And even then, God listens.

Healing, for me, hasn't started with polished prayers. It has started with presence. It looks like tears interrupting sentences. It looks like prayers that sound like breathing. It looks like journal pages that swing from gratitude to frustration. It looks like worship soaked in weeping. It looks like quiet walks where the air becomes my prayer.

And that was the beginning of lament for me. Not the kind I grew up imagining, the kind wrapped in hymns or spoken in a steady voice, but the kind that starts with telling the truth and letting God meet me there. Job's wife showed me I didn't have to hide what hurt or tidy anything up before bringing it to Him. Her story gave me permission to speak from the deepest place within me, the place I was sure would make God look at me differently.

Honesty with God has been sitting in the ashes and trusting He can hold the truth I'd rather hide. When I finally poured out my heart, even the unraveling parts, I found just enough room for comfort to slip in. Little by little, I learned that faith and lament can stand side by side. Faith isn't pretending everything is fine. Faith is believing God is still good even when life isn't. Lament isn't the absence of belief. It is belief refusing to be silent.

And somewhere in that tension, somewhere in that unfiltered honesty, I discovered something sacred. My grief could be honest and holy in the same breath.

When I finally handed Him the emotions I had tried to swallow, something shifted. I wasn't trading my pain for quick comfort. I was letting go of the polished version of myself I kept trying to offer, and that made room for Him to gently anchor me in what was real. A beautiful exchange, if you will.

Lament became the space where I told Him the truth so He could steady me with His.

I didn't wake up the next day healed. Nothing magical happened in my circumstances. I was still grieving my father, and my marriage was still over. But something in me had more room to breathe. Grief didn't feel like a test I was failing anymore. It felt like a place where God kept sitting with me, even when I didn't know what to say next. I started to trust that He could hold the parts of me I used to hide, that He wasn't threatened by my questions or worn out by my tears.

And that's the gift Job's wife left me with. She reminds me that honesty isn't the opposite of faith. Sometimes it's the doorway back to it. My prayers are still imperfect. My heart still aches. But I'm learning that I don't have to come to God cleaned up or composed. I just have to come. And somehow, in that bare and honest space, He keeps meeting me in ways I never expect, slowly turning the loud ache inside me into something steadier, something I can stand on again.

PSALM 23:4

Even though I walk through the valley of the shadow of death, I will fear no evil, for you are with me. Your rod and your staff, they comfort me.

Through the Valley

A Verse to Hold

"Even though I walk through the [sunless] valley of the shadow of death, I fear no evil, for You are with me; Your rod [to protect] and Your staff [to guide], they comfort and console me."

Psalm 23:4 (AMP)

Grief has a way of turning life into a valley that feels endless. Everything changes. Light that once felt warm now feels distant. Mornings that once held promise now arrive with heaviness. The world keeps spinning while yours stands still, and the valley stretches longer than you thought possible.

I used to read Psalm 23 as a gentle promise, something soft and peaceful. Quiet waters. Green pastures. Comforting imagery. But grief changes the way you hear Scripture. Suddenly the valley of the shadow of death is not poetic. It is the place you wake up in. Words about fear and comfort shift from metaphor to survival.

If you have ever walked through that valley, you know how long the darkness can linger. You want to believe God is close, but everything feels muted. Your prayers feel quiet. Your songs feel thin. Even the memories feel far away. Still, within the ache sits a small, steady truth: the Shepherd never leaves. He is not calling out from a mountaintop expecting you to climb out on your own. He is walking with you in the dark, step by step, never letting you move without His presence.

And He is not walking empty-handed. Psalm 23 says He carries a rod and a staff. The rod protects. The staff guides. One defends you from what you cannot see. The other pulls you close when you begin to drift. Even in the valley, you are guarded and guided.

Grief tells you the valley is forever, but God calls it a place you *go through*. Through means movement. Through means there is another side. The ache may linger, but it will not consume you. Even here, God's light is present, and you are gradually becoming able to perceive it once more. Lift your eyes, even if only a little. You may not be on the mountaintop yet, but God's grace is sustaining you right where you stand. Every tear is noticed. Every step is counted. Every moment in the valley is covered by His nearness.

Talk to God

One of the ways we survive the valley is by learning to talk with God there. It is easy to talk about God when life feels good, blessings are visible, and prayers come quickly. Talking to God is different. It means coming without the polished words we use with others. It means letting honesty speak louder than performance. It means bringing the raw, unfiltered parts of your heart and trusting He will not turn away.

Grief tempts you to go quiet. It whispers that God is far, that silence is safer, that people want polished faith and not your broken heart. But God has never asked you to pretend. He asks you to come. Talking to God in the valley turns belief into relationship. Faith shifts from script to conversation—from rehearsed prayers to gut-level honesty, from what you are supposed to say to what you desperately need to scream.

This kind of prayer often sounds like lament.

God, I know You are good, but this still hurts.

I trust You, but I do not understand.

I believe You are here, but I feel alone.

These are not weak prayers. They are sacred. Lament is not a lack of faith. It is faith holding on while everything else falls apart. You do not have to clean up your feelings or filter your tears. You can bring your questions, your anger, your confusion, and He will still listen. Honest prayer does not end the valley, but it brings light into it.

If you learn to talk to God while grieving, your conversations become intimate communion, deep fellowship with Him in your pain. The valley becomes a meeting place. Your pain rests against His peace. Your questions lean into His compassion. Your tears are caught by His tenderness.

Today, shift the conversation. Do not just talk about God. Talk to Him. Tell Him what hurts. Tell Him what you miss. Tell Him how heavy the next step feels. Sit long enough to sense that He is listening. He is not distant or offended by your honesty.

He is near. He is steady. He is guiding you through the valley until you rise again.

In Prayer

Lord, I do not understand everything, but I choose to trust You. I choose to believe that this valley is not forever and that You are guiding me through. Thank You for being near. Thank You for seeing every tear. Thank You for staying with me even in the hardest places. Amen.

Sit with this

What feels hardest to talk to God about right now? Why is it hard to bring that truth to Him?

What parts of my grief or my story do I avoid naming? What am I afraid will happen if I speak them out loud?

Whose Prayer Did You Answer?

A Reflection

So we're back in the garden. I chose gardening as a new hobby this season because it was his. My father worked as a landscaper on the side, and when I was younger, I helped him with smaller flowerbed jobs. Being in the dirt felt like being near him, like I could still reach across the distance between us through something as simple as soil and roots.

I never wore gardening gloves. I probably should have, but I never saw my dad wear them unless he was dealing with rocks or something that could puncture his fingers. So letting the dirt run through my fingers felt like a way to stay connected. It settled under my nails, and somehow that made me feel grounded. Present. A little more like Perry's daughter.

But if I'm honest, gardening wasn't just about connection. It was also about distraction. I had just moved into a new house, one that was supposed to hold a different future, one that was meant for two. Now it was just me, surrounded by empty rooms and the weight of a marriage that had fallen apart. The garden gave me somewhere to put all that restless, aching energy. If I was outside pulling weeds or pruning hydrangeas, I didn't have to sit with the grief. I didn't have to feel the full weight of losing both my father and my husband within days of each other.

We do that, don't we? We reach for things, good things, even pure things, to keep ourselves moving so we don't have to stop and feel what's actually happening on the inside. Sometimes it's work. Sometimes it's the gym. Sometimes it's staying so busy helping everyone else that we never have to face our own unraveling. For me, it was the garden. I would spend hours outside, past the point of necessity, trimming things that didn't need trimming, replanting things that were fine where they were, unnecessary trips to Lowe's, and anything to avoid going back inside to the quiet.

Over time, the garden shifted from distraction to something else. I told you the gun range became the spot where I let my anger burn off. The garden became the opposite. It became my quiet place. The place where my hands could move slowly across the flowers and give God room to remind me who He is. It was where I whispered the questions I didn't know how to pray out loud.

Maybe that's God's grace, that even the things we use to avoid Him can become the very places where He meets us. He's patient like that. He lets us run until we're tired. He lets us distract ourselves until we're ready to sit still. And when we finally do, He's been there the whole time, waiting.

By this point, I had coaxed my bushes into growing the way they were supposed to. I had learned how to trim my hydrangeas so they would give me new blooms. I even bought fancy products to control the weeds. And yet on this particular day, here I was, pulling them up by hand because HOA Hannah decided to bless me with another love letter saying my garden was overgrown. She stayed employed during my grief season, let me tell you.

On this particular day, the why question showed up again.

I was kneeling in the dirt, hands deep in the soil, asking God the question I had asked a hundred times before: *Why didn't You heal him?*

Why didn't we see the miracle so many others had witnessed in their bodies? Why didn't my father get the story that turns around at the last minute? I know God doesn't owe me answers. I know that. But I still asked. I asked again because that's what grief does. That's His invitation in His word.

We gave it everything. We fasted. We pleaded. Our chosen families prayed. We begged heaven to intervene. And still, he died.

So there, with soil on my palms and the sun warming my back, I asked Him one more time: *Why didn't You heal him?*

And then, quietly, a question rose in my spirit that I hadn't expected: *What if healing came, and you just couldn't see it?*

I froze.

My hands stilled in the dirt. My breath caught.

That question rearranged something in me.

I had been so focused on what healing looked like *here*—him staying, us getting more time, the miracle we could witness. But what if healing had come, just not in the way I could see? What if the pain that had worn his body down was gone? What if he was whole in a way he never could have been here?

I sat back on my heels, dirt smudged across my hands, tears falling hot and fast.

I don't know what my father prayed in those final days. I'll never know. But I know his body was tired. I know the pain was real.

We prayed for him to be healed here, where we could see it, where we could celebrate it with him. But his healing came on the other side, in a completeness I can't fully understand from where I'm kneeling. God's ways are higher than mine. And my father is no longer in pain. That is an answered prayer, even if I don't get to witness it. Even if it breaks my heart that he experienced his healing without me.

I don't know if you've ever had a moment where grief cracks open just enough for a sliver of light to slip in. Not enough to make everything okay. Not enough to stop the ache. Just enough to breathe a little deeper.

That was this moment for me.

Healing had come. It simply didn't look the way we hoped.

It didn't erase the longing. I wanted more time. I wanted him to call and hear him say, "Hey, T-Town, this is your dad." But something shifted. The why that had been sitting like a stone in my chest began to soften.

And maybe that's what I couldn't see from where I was kneeling. I was looking at healing from the earthly side of loss. I was grieving the brokenness of his departure from this life. My father was experiencing it from the side of complete wholeness in God.

Because if healing had looked the way I wanted—him staying here with us—what would that have meant? More pain for him. More years of a body that was breaking down. More exhaustion. More fighting. Would I have wanted that for him just so I could keep him a little longer? I want to say no. But if I'm honest, some days the answer is yes. Because grief can be selfish like that. It wants what it wants, and it doesn't care about theology or eternity or who prayed what. It just wants the person back.

But faith asks something different. Faith asks: Can I trust that God's ways are higher, even when I can't see the whole picture? Can I trust that healing came, even when it broke my heart that I couldn't witness it?

I'm still learning how to say yes to that, but it's getting easier.

There's a verse in Job that I used to skip over because it felt too hard. After Job learns he has lost everything, he doesn't collapse into silence. He says this:

"The Lord gave and the Lord has taken away; may the name of the Lord be praised." (Job 1:21, NIV).

For a long time, I thought that verse was about surrender. And it is. But now I think it's also about trust. Trust that the same God who gives life also holds death. Trust that His decisions, even the ones that devastate us, are still woven with love. I know I told you before that I understand Job's wife more than I understand Job. I'm Mrs. Job, remember? Most days, I'm still wrestling. Still asking. Still kneeling in the dirt with questions that don't have clean answers. But there' s a little Job in me too.

That day in the garden, I learned something I didn't expect: God is not threatened by me asking why. He's big enough to hold that question and me. And sometimes, instead of giving me the answer I think I need, He gives me a different perspective, one that opens a door I didn't know was there.

What if healing came, and you just couldn't see it?

I know the ache of missing my dad will never completely fade. But I'm starting to see that even though healing doesn't always look like what we pray for, sometimes it looks like freedom from pain. Sometimes it looks like wholeness we can't witness from this side of heaven.

I kneeled in the garden a while longer, letting the tears come. Then I wiped my face, took a breath, and went back to pulling weeds. The garden still needed tending. My hands moved through the soil, mentally tracing where I would plant my next round of flowers, and something about this felt different now. Steadier. Like there was something I didn't have to carry anymore.

I thought about the lilies scripture in Matthew 6, how God clothes them even though they're only here for a moment. How they don't worry about tomorrow because they're held today. And I realized: my father was held too. In every season of his life, through every moment of his illness, God's attention never wavered. He was cared for then, beautifully, tenderly. And he's cared for now.

I didn't get the miracle I begged for. But kneeling there in the dirt, I understood that the question wasn't whether God loved my father enough to heal him. It was whether I could trust that God's care for him, then and now, was enough. Even when it didn't look the way I wanted it to.

And somehow, that felt true for me too. My grief wasn't gone, but the silent worry beneath it, the one I hadn't even named, began to ease. I didn't have to keep asking if my father was okay. He was held.

And that's what faith looks like: not certainty about the answers we'll get, but trust in the One who holds both sides of the story.

When the sun started to set, I went inside. The house was still quiet. The grief was still there. But so was something else. A small, tender knowing that I could give this to God and trust that His ways are higher than mine, even when I don't understand.

I may always wrestle with the miracle we didn't see. But I'm learning that trust doesn't require understanding. It requires surrender. Surrender to a God who sees what I cannot, who holds what I'm grieving in one hand and the healing I cannot witness in the other.

Some days, that surrender feels like peace. Other days, it feels like survival. But either way, it's enough.

I'm learning that some of the holiest moments happen with dirt under your nails and tears on your cheeks, when you're brave enough to ask the hard questions and trust God with the answers you may never fully understand

My father is healed. This grief will last for a very long time. And God holds both my heartbreak and my father's healing with the same sovereign hands.

July 14, 2024

I just don't understand.

And maybe I never will.

Everybody says it gets better, but I don't even know what better means anymore. Because this? I can't even go to the store without being reminded of my dad and bursting into tears. People talk about "moving on," but what does that even look like? How do you move on from someone who was part of you?

I'm tired of trying to make it make sense. It doesn't. It never will. I still catch myself wanting to call, to share something funny, to hear his voice. Then it hits me that I can't. And I can't even call my husband because I am so damn angry.

This isn't fair, and I will never understand it. I am not perfect, God, but I didn't deserve this.

But God I know you good. I know you are good. I've seen it before. I know you are good. Help me to believe that you are good.

When Hope Whispers Back

A Verse to Hold

"Yet this I call to mind and therefore I have hope: Because of the Lord's great love we are not consumed, for his compassions never fail."

Lamentations 3:21–22 (NIV)

Can I ask you something honest? Have you ever felt like sadness made you a problem in certain Christian circles? Like you were expected to be "fine" before you even had the chance to fall apart? I know that feeling too well. Grief can make you feel like your emotions need permission slips before you bring them into certain spaces.

But this verse from Lamentations tells a different story. Jeremiah was surrounded by ruin. His city was in pieces. His heart was shattered. And right in the middle of that devastation, he prayed the most honest words he had. He told God the truth about the sorrow and suffering he was experiencing: *"I well remember them, and my soul is downcast within me."* He lamented until he had nothing left to say. Then, almost like a breath, he remembered something.

Yet this I call to mind and therefore I have hope.

It was not strength. It was not clarity. It was memory. He remembered that God's love had not failed him, that grief had not consumed him, that compassion still arrived every morning, even when hope felt thin.

That is what lament does. It makes space for your grief to breathe until hope can find its way back in.

Lament is not the absence of faith. It is what faith sounds like when your heart is cracked open. Real faith has edges. It trembles. It cries. It asks questions that feel too heavy to say out loud. And God is not put off by any of that. He is not waiting for you to compose yourself before He leans in. Pretending might convince people you are okay, but honesty is what brings God close.

Lament is conversation, not performance. You do not have to explain your pain to God. You simply place it in His hands, raw and unfinished. That is exactly what Jeremiah did. He spoke from the rubble. He did not edit his sadness or hide his confusion. And in the very middle of grief, he found hope rising again because he remembered who God had been all along.

Even Jesus wept when His people were grieving. He knew resurrection was coming, yet He still allowed Himself to feel the weight of their pain. If Jesus makes space for tears, you can too. Your sadness is not unspiritual. Your questions are not a threat to God. Your tears are holy.

So if you are sitting in a dark place right now, do not rush yourself. Grief takes time. Healing takes time. God is not tapping His foot waiting for you to pull it together. He is sitting beside you, steady and patient, being the light for you until you are able to hope again.

And hope will return. It rarely arrives with fireworks. Most days it slips in quietly, like the smell of coffee at sunrise. You might notice it as a breath you did not think you could take, a moment of strength you did not expect, a text you did not know you needed. Hope returns in small ways, while your heart is still tender, while you are still unsure.

And when it does, it will not demand that you be perfect. It will simply remind you of what Jeremiah remembered: you are not consumed. You are not abandoned. God's compassion has not failed you.

In Prayer

You see the places in me that ache, the parts I hide from others, and the heaviness I can barely put into words. Thank You that Your compassion has not run out. Thank You that I am not consumed, even on the days when I feel like I am unraveling. Thank You that Your love stays steady when everything else feels fragile. Amen.

Sit with this

Take some time to lament. Write out all the thoughts you are afraid to give to people.

Where do you find it hardest to allow yourself to be honest with God about what hurts?

What small, quiet ways has hope shown up for you in this season, even when you didn't recognize it at first?

The Helper Who Knows Your Language

A Verse to Hold

"But I tell you the truth, it is to your advantage that I go away. For if I do not go away, the Helper will not come to you. But if I go, I will send Him to you to be in close fellowship with you."

John 16:7 (AMP)

When Jesus spoke these words, the disciples were heartbroken. They could not imagine anything good coming from His absence. They could only feel what they were losing. They did not yet understand what they would gain—that the Holy Spirit would bring a different kind of closeness. Not replacing Jesus, but carrying His presence to each of them personally, wherever they went, forever.

The Spirit would dwell within them, knowing them from the inside. He would comfort them in personal ways. He would speak their language.

Grief has a way of making your world feel small and hard to reach. No one else knows the exact memories you lost or the private jokes that shaped your bond. People can hold your hands, but they cannot always hold your heart. And that is where the gift of the Holy Spirit becomes something more than a doctrine. It becomes breath. It becomes presence. It becomes the kind of comfort no human can offer.

Jesus knew how loneliness felt. He knew the ache of leaving people He loved. He also knew the only way His friends would survive the coming loss was through the presence of someone who could reach them in places even He, in human form, could not.

That is what the Holy Spirit does for us now. He steps into the quiet. He sits in the empty spaces of grief. He speaks to us in ways so personal, so gentle, so specific, that no one else would even recognize it as comfort. But you know. Your heart knows.

Sometimes He comforts through a memory that brings peace instead of pain. Sometimes through a dream. Sometimes through unexpected moments of strength, a Scripture that suddenly speaks to your specific hurt, or a friend's perfectly timed presence. Not a coincidence. Not manufactured. Just the Holy Spirit knowing exactly how to reach you in the language your grief still understands.

The Spirit is not a distant helper. He is a close companion. Jesus called Him Comforter, Advocate, Counselor, Strengthener, and Standby. Every name speaks to a different need. Every title is a promise that you are not walking through your grief without support. His presence does not erase the pain, but it keeps the pain from erasing you.

If you feel alone, you are not forgotten. If you feel misunderstood, you are still known. If you feel like the world has moved on, God has not.

You can talk to the Holy Spirit in the same honest language you spoke with the person you lost. He can handle your confusion, your questions, your anger, and the places that feel tender. He responds not with pressure to *move on* but with presence that lets you heal. He stays until your breath steadies and your heart remembers you are not walking through this valley alone.

Today, let this truth settle in your bones. Jesus left so the Spirit could come close. Closer than breath. Closer than memory. Not beside you, but within you. Closer than any comfort this world can offer.

And He still knows how to speak the language that reaches you.

In Prayer

God, thank You for being near when I feel unseen. When no one else seems to understand, remind me that You do. Help me rest in Your presence and trust that You are holding both my tears and my healing. Show me that You are here and that You see me. Amen

Sit with this

Think of a time when you felt unseen or misunderstood in your grief. How might you invite God into that space and allow His presence to comfort you there?

What Do We Do Now?

A Reflection

The night my father passed, Uncle Ken and I stood in the hospital lobby under fluorescent lights that made everything feel slightly unreal. He had done this before. More times than anyone should have to. It is true what people say. One sibling ends up at every funeral. One ends up at none. He was the youngest of ten. Only three were left now.

Through tears, we asked him, "What do we do now?" He did not offer a sermon or a plan. Just a steady voice that said, "You go home, and I'll see y'all tomorrow."

That was it. That was all he had.

People who know this grief don't hand you answers because they understand answers won't help. They give you instructions small enough to carry. Go home. Breathe. Get through the night.

Before we left the hospital, I sent texts to a few close friends because I knew they would show up, and I knew I would need them. Then we went home and sat in my parents' living room, wrapped in a silence that felt heavier than words. None of us knew what came next. We just stayed together.

Grief rearranges everything. What you thought you knew about God. About love. About time. It interrupts your rhythms and leaves you standing still while the world keeps moving.

My sister and I had moved back home a few years earlier. I was newly married. We had plans. Trips. Holidays. A future that assumed my dad would be here. We had learned the rhythm of caregiving and were quietly holding out hope for a miracle. If God healed him, everything could still happen. Even if it looked different, at least he would be with us. When that rhythm ended, it felt like music stopping mid-song. Sudden. Hollow. Disorienting.

After the first few weeks, the noise faded. Paperwork got done. Services ended. The chicken stopped coming. The texts slowed down. But his cup was still on the end table by his recliner. The house still smelled like him.

Doctors kept calling. Appointment reminders. Follow-ups. Each time we had to explain that he was gone. There was no system that told everyone at once. Every call felt like being thrown backwards in the same moment we were trying to survive.

That is when the fog started settling in. It came low and slow, like early morning mist spreading across a field. At first, I could still see the shape of my days. I answered messages. Sat in familiar rooms. From the outside, I looked steady.

Then the fog thickened. As if losing my father was not disorienting enough, another loss was unfolding quietly at the same time. My husband and I were in the early days of separation. Nothing dramatic. No final papers signed yet. Just distance. Silence. Conversations that circled the same wounds without landing anywhere safe. Losing my father had already taken away one place of belonging. Now the future I had built inside my marriage felt uncertain too. I was not only grieving who I had lost. I was grieving who I thought I would become.

Months passed. Depression slipped in quietly. I lived on the couch. Ate whatever I could order. Gained weight I do not love to number. I had just joined a fitness bootcamp the week my dad died. When I finally went back, I tried to push through because that is what people kept telling me to do. Halfway through the workout, my body refused, and I broke down and went home. After that, home became the only place that felt safe.

We were all grieving the same loss, but not in the same way. We were standing in the same fog, but we weren't facing the same direction. My mother had lost her partner. Her person. The one who knew where everything was kept and what she looked like at twenty-two. Her fog was facing a future that came sooner than she wanted. My siblings and I had lost our father.

But even that wasn't the same loss, because we didn't have the same father. We each had a version of him that belonged to us alone. The dad who taught one of us to drive. The one who showed up at the game. The one who said the hard thing or didn't. We were grieving different a man who wore the same face. So even standing side by side, we were moving in different directions without knowing it.

That's what no one tells you about shared grief. It isn't actually shared. It's parallel. You're each carrying something that only has your name on it, trying to hold the door open for each other when your hands are just as full. My fog was the kind you don't drive in. The kind where you pull over and wait for it to lift. But someone else's fog was just a haze, uncomfortable, yes, but passable. We kept looking at each other across the same grief, wondering why we weren't moving at the same pace. Some days I reminded myself I wasn't navigating just one thing. Grieving my father was heavy. Grieving the slow unraveling of my marriage made the air feel almost unbreathable.

Eventually the fog shifted. Not into clarity, but into questions. *Maybe if I had prayed differently. Maybe if we had noticed something sooner. Maybe if God had answered the way I hoped.* Fog blurs the line between what happened and what might have been. It tempts me to believe there was another version of the story, one where everyone stayed whole. Slowly I began to understand that none of this was something to fix or solve. It was something I just had to find a way through.

By the time I began planning my fortieth birthday, life looked almost normal from the outside. We had gotten through the year of firsts and then some, so it was time for a celebration. I was choosing flowers and linens, imagining a room filled with people I loved. Then the thought arrived quietly and sat beside me. My dad would have loved this. He would have shown up early even after complaining he had to dress up. Hugged everyone. Acted like he had known them forever. I cried over centerpiece ideas, wiped my face, and kept planning.

Fog does not always stop you. Sometimes it simply walks with you. Over time I learned how to move inside it. You do not run in fog. You slow down. You stay close to what is familiar. You trust small landmarks. The sound of a friend's voice. The comfort of routine. The memory of where the road bends. I began to notice that God was not waiting for me on the other side of the fog. He was meeting me within it. In quiet presence. In unexpected strength. In the softness that comes when you finally stop pretending to be fine.

Healing does not arrive as sudden sunlight. It comes as visibility. Ten feet. Then twenty. Then the faint outline of a horizon I am not sure I can trust but keep going.

Some mornings I open the blinds and notice the light does not hurt my eyes anymore. It rests gently on the floor. I stand there longer than usual, letting my vision adjust. Realizing I can finally see far enough to take the next step.

Fog lifts in its own time. Sometimes it returns without warning. But it does not mean you are lost. It means you are still here. Looking back, that season was not wasted. Even when I could not see clearly, God was restoring what had frayed. Teaching me that healing is not the absence of grief, but the presence of grace within it.

So if you find yourself asking, "What do we do now?" the answer may be simpler than you expect. Go home. Rest. Stay close to the people who matter. And when morning comes, open the blinds. Stand still until your eyes adjust. Then take the next small steps you can see.

Help my Heart Catch Up

A Verse to Hold

"for it is God who works in you to will and to act in order to fulfill his good purpose."

Philippians 2:13 NIV

I learned the hardest truth about forgiveness during the season I was breaking in more ways than one. Losing my father. Watching my marriage fall apart only days later. Standing in rooms where grief and betrayal pressed against each other until I could not tell which ache belonged to which. Forgiveness sounds so holy until you have to live it. For a long time, I told myself I had forgiven, but my body knew better. The tension never left. I carried memories like luggage I could not put down. They followed me into conversations, dreams, and even prayer. I convinced myself I was healed because I had stopped talking about it. But silence is not the same as peace. I had only learned how to keep my pain quiet.

People often say, *You have got to forgive so you can move forward.* But when your heart is hurting and the memories still sting, forgiveness can feel less like freedom and more like letting go of the only control you have left. I thought forgiveness meant pretending something did not happen or acting like it did not matter. But pretending is not the same as healing, and minimizing pain does not make it disappear.

Grief made forgiveness even harder. When you lose someone or something you never thought you would lose—whether a marriage, a friendship, or the future you prayed for—forgiveness can feel like another impossible task. You replay everything, wondering what could have been different. Anger shows up dressed as protection, but really, it keeps you tied to the same hurt.

I remember nights when I sat with God and said, *I want to forgive, but I do not know how. This was wrong. It was unfair.* Part of me believed that surely I did not have to forgive something like that. My anger felt justified—and in some ways it was. But I was learning there is a difference between righteous anger at sin and the kind of unforgiveness that consumes and embitters us.

Ephesians 4:31–32 says, *"Get rid of all bitterness, rage, and anger… forgiving each other, just as in Christ God forgave you."* I knew this verse well, but living it felt impossible. That is when Philippians 2:13 became a lifeline: *"God is working in you, giving you the desire and the power to do what pleases Him."* I did not have to pretend to be okay with forgiveness. I just needed to be honest. Even if my only prayer was, *Help me want to,* that was enough for God to begin.

Forgiveness is not one big spiritual moment. It is a slow journey back to peace. It happens in small ways: when you stop replaying the same conversations, when you pray for healing instead of answers, when you stop needing to win the story in your mind. Each time, the burden gets a little lighter.

Jesus shows us this slow, costly forgiveness when He prayed for the ones who made His cross, asking the Father to forgive them even as they drove in the nails. That prayer cost Him something. Forgiveness always costs something: it cost Jesus His life, and it costs us our right to bitterness and revenge. But what we gain is freedom—the door opened for what only God can do: resurrection, restoration, and a peace that cannot be explained.

Holding on to unforgiveness is a heavy burden. Sometimes you do not notice it at first. It becomes exhausting. It becomes bitterness you cannot name. It becomes distance between you and God. Resentment fills the space that God wants to heal. And while God can meet you anywhere, He will not force your hands open.

But here is what forgiveness actually is, and what it is not.

Forgiveness does not always lead to reconciliation. You can forgive someone and still maintain boundaries. You can release bitterness and still acknowledge broken trust. Forgiveness sets you free. It does not obligate you to restore what was not safe.

And forgiveness is not the same as forgetting. Forgetting is passive, often impossible, and sometimes unwise. Forgiveness is active. It is the daily choice to carry the memory without letting it become a weapon.

When Peter asked Jesus how many times to forgive, Jesus replied, *"Not seven times, but seventy times seven."* He was not giving a number. He was describing a rhythm. A lifestyle. A way of living free. And when you begin to live in that rhythm, something shifts. Forgiveness does not erase what happened, but it changes what comes next. It makes room in your heart for peace to return. It frees up space for joy that grief buried.

And when forgiveness feels impossible, the most honest prayer you can pray is, *God, I want to forgive them. Please help my heart catch up.* That is where healing begins. Not when everything is fixed, but when you say, *God, I am ready for You to help me let go.* And when you do, something shifts. You realize forgiveness was never about releasing them from debt. It was about releasing yourself from carrying it.

In Prayer

God, I bring You the hurt I have been carrying and the anger that will not let go. Help me want to forgive, even when everything in me resists. Give me the desire and the power to release what was done to me—not because it did not matter, but because I do not want bitterness to consume me. Teach me that forgiveness does not mean pretending or reconciling. It means setting myself free. When my heart lags behind my will, be patient with me and keep working in me. I choose to trust You with what I cannot yet release. Amen.

Sit with this

How might forgiveness open space for peace in your life right now?

What would it look like to pray, "Lord, *help me want to forgive*?"

Take me Through There

A Verse to Hold

"You make known to me the path of life; you will fill me with joy in your presence, with eternal pleasures at your right hand."

Psalm 16:11 (NIV)

When you are in the middle of grief or uncertainty, your mind can easily wander to the *what ifs*. What if things had gone another way. What if I had done more. What if I never feel whole again. These questions can spin in circles until you are exhausted and still searching for peace.

But what if, somewhere in the middle of unanswered questions, the questions themselves could shift? Not *what if* or *why,* but *which way*. Which way does God want us to go from here? Which way helps us live when we can barely think past the next sunrise?

Asking which way did not erase the pain. It simply made room for God to guide the next small step instead of expecting us to see the entire road at once.

Psalm 16:11 says, *"You make known to me the path of life."* I used to think that meant God would hand me a clear map, but healing taught me that this path is a daily invitation. It is not a secret trail for the strong. It is for the tired, the discouraged, the ones who are still learning how to trust. Some days the road feels dark and you can barely see what is next. That is when you most need His Spirit as a lamp for your feet. Not a floodlight for the future, just enough light to keep you moving. It is His way of saying, *You do not have to carry tomorrow. Just walk with Me today.*

And when you shift from asking why this way to which way, Lord, something begins to soften inside you. Your eyes open to His presence in small, ordinary moments. A conversation that arrives on the exact day you need encouragement. A verse that settles your spirit. A song that steadies your breath at the red light. A quiet mercy that reminds you God has not forgotten you. The journey stops feeling like a test you are failing and becomes what it always was, a walk with a Father who knows where He is leading you.

It is in this slow walk that joy begins to return. Not loud joy. Not the kind that demands a celebration. David wrote, *"You will fill me with joy in Your presence."* Sometimes that joy is simply a deep exhale when you realize you survived a day you thought would break you. Sometimes it is the warmth that comes from knowing you have not walked alone. It is subtle, but it is real.

The psalm ends with a promise that stretches far beyond the moment: *"With eternal pleasures at Your right hand."* David is reminding us that God's goodness is not confined to outcomes in this life. It reaches into eternity. What God offers is not a guarantee that everything on earth will resolve the way we pray, but a certainty that His presence and His joy will carry us beyond every earthly sorrow. His right hand is where our souls remember that pain is temporary and His glory is not. And when that eternal truth begins to anchor you, the *what ifs* lose their authority, and your heart becomes steady enough to ask with peace, *which way now, Lord.*

And when God shows you the path of life, He is not asking you to leave behind what broke your heart. He is inviting you to move forward with it. That is different. Moving forward means carrying both love and pain, not as a burden, but as something precious you hold close. It is the quiet courage to rise again. It is the gentle strength to take another step even when the path feels unfamiliar without the person or season you lost. It is softly asking, *Lord, which way now?* and trusting that He walks each step with you.

There is no timeline for this. There is no performance required. Just the next step with the light you have, trusting that the same God who met you in sorrow will walk beside you in renewal.

In Prayer

Father, Thank You for being near, even when the road feels long and uncertain. Teach my heart to ask not why but which way. Lead me through the places that still ache, through the moments I do not understand, and through the quiet spaces where Your presence becomes my peace. Amen.

Sit with this

What are the *What ifs* that keep replaying in your mind? How might you surrender them and instead ask God, *Which way?*

Where in your current season do you sense God inviting you to trust Him more deeply, even when the path is unclear?

Oh Man, My Dimes

A Reflection

Loneliness in grief has its own pulse. It is the ache of being surrounded by people and still feeling like no one speaks the language you lost. People check in. They bring food. They pray. They call you strong. And you appreciate it, but there is still a part of you that feels stranded between the before and after, clutching memories no one else knows how to translate. Loneliness in grief is not so much about being alone as it is about being misunderstood. There were days when the house felt full and still somehow hollow, like I could hear the echo of what used to be.

Part of what deepens that loneliness is the simple truth that every relationship has its own vocabulary. The tiny jokes. The shared glances. The rhythms that belong to just the two of you. When the person is gone, the language breaks in your hands. Suddenly the world feels too loud and too quiet at the same time. You start reaching for words that no longer have a place to land.

My dad and I had a language like that, and one of our favorite phrases in it was, "Oh man, my dimes!" It sounds simple when I say it now, but that was what made it sacred.

Love hides in small corners and somehow those corners become everything.

It started the summer before he passed. My older sister had also moved back home after twenty years in the military, which already felt surreal. We hadn't lived in the same city since I was a teenager. The three of us were in the car running errands, getting used to being a full family again in ways that felt both new and familiar. My sister drove. Dad sat in the passenger seat. I was in the back watching them bicker and bond like no time had passed.

We pulled up to a four-way stop where volunteer firefighters were standing in the intersection collecting donations. My dad was famous for keeping loose change. He treated quarters and dimes like they were precious metals. Any time you got in his car, you could hear them clinking around, tucked into every cup holder and crevice like they were tiny savings accounts.

When we approached the intersection, my sister did something that would go down in family history. Without hesitation, she scooped up every single coin in the console and handed the whole handful to the firefighter. It had to be at least five or six dollars' worth. She didn't even look at Dad when she did it.

My dad turned to her with the most offended expression, mouth open, eyes wide, like she had just given away a family heirloom. He exclaimed, "Oh man, my dimes!" He said it the way someone might say, "Oh man, my life's work."

And without missing a beat, without even glancing his way, my sister said, "Man, if you don't shut up about some dimes."

The timing was perfect. The delivery was deadly. The moment hit all three of us at once, and we cracked up. It was the kind of laugh that makes your stomach hurt. A laugh that marks you. After that, "my dimes" became our shared language. Whenever I had spare change, I would pass it to my dad and say, "Here, Dad, here are your dimes," and he would grin like I had given him something priceless. It was our thing. Small but sacred.

After he passed, that language felt broken. I kept reaching for it without realizing it was gone.

Then the dreams started.

I had soft dreams where we were together again. In one of them, we were back in the car laughing about the dimes like nothing had shifted. His laugh in that dream felt so real and so close that waking up felt like losing him twice.

One night after that dream, I woke up crying. Not dramatic tears. Just a slow and quiet unraveling. I felt this gentle nudge in my spirit, almost like a whisper saying, "Get up." It was two in the morning. The house was still. The day had already been heavy. At the time, I lived in the new phase of a neighborhood that was still developing. There were no houses in front of mine yet, just an open field and an unobstructed stretch of sky. On nights when sleep would not hold me, I would sometimes go outside and sit in the driveway just to look at the stars and breathe.

My garage was still full of boxes from the move, so I kept my car parked in the driveway. That night, when I stepped outside, I told myself I was going to move the car so I could sit cleanly in the open space. It sounded practical enough.

I opened my car door, and as I stepped back, something caught the corner of my eye. I looked down and saw a single dime on the ground right beside my foot.

Maybe it had fallen earlier. Maybe it had been there for days. There are a hundred logical explanations. But grief does not operate in logic. Grief lives in meaning and notices what the heart is ready to see.

And in that moment, that tiny dime felt like oxygen. It felt like God saying, "I see you. I know what this joke meant. I know the ache beneath it. I am closer than you think."

Not a voice from the sky.

Not a dramatic sign.

Just a dime in the driveway at two in the morning holding a language only my heart spoke.

Sometimes comfort arrives exactly like that.

Small.

Quiet.

Tender.

A whisper that reaches you in the place where words cannot.

What I did not understand in those early months was how much of the ache came from feeling like no one could meet me where I was. People cared. They tried. But there are places in grief where human closeness cannot reach. Places too tender, too disoriented, too wordless. I kept looking for someone who could understand the space inside me that nothing seemed to fill.

Over time, I began to see that God reached for me long before I ever reached for Him. Those small signs and unexpected comforts were not random. They were reminders that He knew the contours of my grief better than anyone around me. He recognized the language even when I could not speak it out loud.

I used to think moving forward meant getting stronger or feeling less broken or learning how to leave the hardest parts behind. But moving forward started to look different than I expected. It looked like walking with the One who was already beside me. It looked like noticing the gentle ways He kept showing up, not to erase the pain but to sit with me in it. A dime in the driveway. A familiar laugh in a dream. A moment of peace that felt like borrowed strength.

None of it fixed the loss. None of it stitched everything back together. But this small wonder taught me something I could not learn any other way. It taught me that God meets me in the places where words fail and where no one else can stand with me. It taught me that His presence is not distant or theoretical. It is close. Personal. Attentive.

And this is how I keep going. Not by outrunning the grief or pretending it weighs less, but by letting these quiet miracles guide me forward. Step by step. Day by day. Dime by dime. Until the path itself starts to feel like companionship. Until the nearness of God becomes the steady thing I lean on as I journey toward the place where everything broken is finally made whole.

Through the Fire

A Verse to Hold

"and provide for those who grieve in Zion— to bestow on them a crown of beauty instead of ashes, the oil of joy instead of mourning, and a garment of praise instead of a spirit of despair. They will be called oaks of righteousness, a planting of the Lord for the display of his splendor."

Isaiah 61:3 (NIV)

After the chaos, the phone calls, the tears, and the quiet, when the noise finally fades, something unexpected happens. A stillness settles in. Not peace, not yet. More like a pause that forces you to feel how loud grief has been inside you. Maybe you know that moment. After the loss. After the ending. After the news that changed everything. Life keeps moving, but you cannot. You are surrounded by the ashes of what used to be, whispering, *What do I do now?*

In Scripture, ashes were never meaningless. They represented real devastation, real loss. And God did not dismiss them. He met people in their ashes and promised exchange: beauty for ashes, joy for mourning. Your grief is seen. Your hope is secure. God does not ask you to pretend the ashes are not there. He does not wait for you to sweep them away before He comes close. He sits with you in the dust because ashes are the place where He begins His rebuilding.

I remember sitting in my living room one night when the house was quiet and the weight of grief felt louder than my breath. It was not only the ache of losing my dad. Another grief had been threading through my days too. My marriage had been unraveling for a long time. Betrayal had broken what I kept trying to hold together with hope and prayer and effort. But that night, something inside me shifted. I realized I had been carrying a burden God never asked me to carry alone. I had been trying to control outcomes I could not change, fix what was shattered by someone else's choices, and manufacture healing through sheer will. In that stillness, I surrendered the ashes of my marriage—not the commitment itself, but the desperate attempt to orchestrate an outcome only God could bring. I laid my need for control at His feet, my fear of what might come, my white-knuckled determination to hold together something that had already burned down. It broke me to release that burden. The marriage would eventually end, and that brought its own devastating grief. But that night was when I stopped trying to be God in a situation where I could only be human—faithful, heartbroken, and dependent on Him to carry what I could not.

Isaiah 61:3 is not about quick exchanges. It is a slow, sacred transformation. A crown of beauty instead of ashes, beauty that grows out of the very places that burned, not because the burning was good, but because God's redemption is that powerful. The oil of joy instead of mourning, joy that rises gently from deep wounds. A garment of praise instead of despair, not praise that performs strength, but praise that whispers, I am still here. And oaks of righteousness. Steady trees that stand tall only because their roots found God in ruined places.

Grief insists the ashes are the end of the story. But God sees them as soil for something new. They are the place where deeper compassion grows, where faith takes root, where hope becomes more honest and more real. God does not rush this. The world may expect quick recoveries, but God moves gently. He restores slowly, the way morning light softens the horizon before it breaks through.

When Isaiah says God will *"bestow"* beauty, joy, and praise, it means He places them on us Himself. We do not have to manufacture strength or force healing or act further along than we are. God gives joy when we cannot find our own. God wraps us in praise when despair tries to settle. God names us oaks when we still feel like dust.

If you are looking at what is left and wondering how to move forward, hear this gently. God is not asking you to figure out the next step alone. He is not distant or waiting for you to get stronger. He is sitting with you in the ashes, shaping something new with His hands.

The beauty He brings does not replace what you lost. It redeems it. It turns your story into something that carries His splendor. Something that says, *I have walked through fire, and God met me there.*

When you do not know what to do next, you do not have to. Just stay close. The same God who breathed life into dust at creation knows how to breathe beauty into your ashes now.

In Prayer

God, You see what's left. You see the ashes I can barely hold. Sit with me here in the quiet where words run out. Teach me not to rush Your work. Let Your beauty rise slowly, and when it does, help me recognize it as You. Amen.

Sit with this

What "ashes" are you holding right now that feel too heavy to release?

What might beauty look like for you in this next season, even if it is small and unseen?

And All the Time

A Verse to Hold

"When Mary reached the place where Jesus was and saw him, she fell at his feet and said, Lord, if you had been here, my brother would not have died. When Jesus saw her weeping, and the Jews who had come along with her also weeping, he was deeply moved in spirit and troubled."

John 11:32-33 (NIV)

There have been seasons when hearing God is good felt complicated. I still believed it, but the belief felt thin. My life was coming apart in places I had begged God to hold together. I would celebrate someone else's miracle and then go home wondering why my own prayers seemed to go silent.

You know those moments. Someone gets the job. Someone gets the clear scan. Someone brings their baby home. The group chat erupts: *Look at God.* And you look. You really do. But deep down you are thinking, *Why not here? Why not me?*

That is where this tension begins. What do you do when the miracle does not come? When there is no healing. No restored relationship. No last-minute rescue. When you are standing at a graveside you prayed would never exist.

I have lived in that ache. Praying like everything depended on it. Meeting silence that felt unbearable. Believing God could do anything and learning that sometimes His will differs from the miracle you begged for most.

That is why Mary's perspective in John 11 always stops me. It holds love and disappointment at once. Mary and Martha send word that Lazarus is sick. They knew what Jesus could do. They had seen Him heal. But this time, Jesus does not rush. By the time He arrives, Lazarus is gone. Mary runs to Him, falls at His feet, and cries out, *"Lord, if You had been here, my brother would not have died."* That line is raw honesty. She believes in His power but cannot reconcile His timing. She loves Him and feels let down at the same time.

And Jesus does not correct her. He does not tell her to trust harder or try to talk her out of her grief. He weeps with her. Before resurrection, there is sorrow. Before answers, there are tears. God does not hurry past our pain, even when we wish He would. He sits in it with us, even when we are desperate for Him to fix it.

I think of nights when my only prayer was, *Where were You?* Nights when everything in my life felt upside down. Nights when I whispered, *If You love me, why does this hurt so much?* I never got explanations. But I did get presence. Not clarity. Not fast healing. Just the kind of nearness that does not leave when everything else does.

And somewhere in that quiet, I learned something I wish I had known sooner. God is good even when His timing feels too late. God is good even when the story does not go the way we begged Him to write it. God is good even when nothing makes sense.

Because His goodness is not tied to the outcome. It is tied to His character: who He is, not what He does. And His character is to stay near, even in the places where nothing gets fixed. Faith is not pretending the pain is small. Faith is trusting He is close, even when your story has gone another way. Sometimes the miracle is not what comes back to life. Sometimes the miracle is that God sustains the part of you that keeps believing while you wait.

We like to measure God's goodness by results, by the things we can point to. But what if the clearest place to see His goodness is in the moments He refuses to walk away? What if He is good because He stays, even when nothing turns out the way we prayed? I still have days when I wish He moved faster or answered differently. But I am learning that His goodness is something deeper than timing. It is presence. It is nearness. It is the steady way He holds us through pain He did not stop.

So maybe the most faithful thing we can do is what Mary did. Fall at His feet. Tell the truth. Let the tears come. And stay long enough to notice that He is weeping too.

And even when it looks too late, even when the story breaks, God is still good. Quietly. Steadily. In ways we are still learning how to see.

In Prayer

Father, thank You for being good even when life is not. Thank You for meeting me in the places where disappointment and faith collide. Help me to trust that Your goodness is not dependent on outcomes, but on Your unchanging nature. When I find myself asking where You are, remind me that You have always been near. Teach me to see Your goodness, even in the waiting. Amen.

Sit with this

When was a time you found yourself asking God, "Where were You?" How did that question shape your understanding of His presence?

What does redefining *good* look like for you in this season of life?

Consider the lilies of the field, how they
grow; they toil not, neither do they spin

Matthew 6:28

When the Lilies Teach Us to Rest

A Verse to Hold

"See how the lilies of the field grow. They do not labor or spin."

Matthew 6:28 (NIV)

When my dad died, I kept asking myself how I was supposed to build a life without him. I had known grief before, but this was different. It was deeper, sharper, and somehow heavier. The same question followed me everywhere I went: *What do we do now?*

What do we do now that he is gone? What do we do now that nothing feels familiar? I tried to answer it by thinking harder, reading more, replaying old memories, searching for some clear stage of grief that would make everything make sense. But grief does not work like that. It refuses to be organized. It does not follow a map. You cannot study your way out of it.

I was sitting in my car one afternoon, too tired to go inside yet, when a friend texted me Jesus' words: *"See how the lilies of the field grow. They do not labor or spin."* I had read that verse a hundred times before and assumed it was only about worry, about unclenching my hands and trusting God with the future. But reading it through tears, in that quiet moment when I had nothing left to give, it sounded different. It felt like an invitation to stop trying to fix what could not be fixed.

In the first days after a loss, you want order. You want something solid to hold. So you work hard to understand what has happened, thinking that if you can name it or categorize it, maybe the pain will ease. But Jesus points to flowers that do none of that. They are held, not because they strive, but because their Father cares for them. The lilies do not work to bloom. They simply receive what they need.

Grief has a way of making us feel exposed. Stripped bare. Like every defense we once had has been torn away and we are standing in an open field with nowhere to hide. The routines that used to steady us feel hollow. The faith that once came easily now feels fragile. We are vulnerable in ways we never expected, and the world keeps moving around us as if nothing has changed.

But here is what Jesus shows us: the lilies stand exposed too. They have no walls, no shelter, no protection from the elements. They are completely at the mercy of sun and wind and rain. And yet God clothes them. He tends to them. He does not leave them bare. God's care does not disappear when our world falls apart. The same God who clothes the fields in spring is the one who cares for us. Renewal still comes after winter. Even when everything looks barren, God is quietly tending to what is unseen.

It is powerful to watch lilies rise after months of cold. The ground that looked lifeless suddenly breaks open with color. That beauty is not accidental. It is rooted in a design that allows growth in hidden places first. For months, nothing is visible. The field looks empty. But beneath the surface, roots are deepening, drawing life from the soil, preparing for what will one day bloom.

Grief feels like that hidden place. Buried. Dark. Forgotten. And yet, even there, God is present. Not because grief is good or because loss is something we needed, but because God does not abandon us in the dark. He stays. He tends. He sustains what we cannot see or feel. And somehow, in ways we may not recognize until much later, He is faithful even when we cannot trace His hand.

Jesus' invitation to *consider the lilies* is not a correction. It is comfort. It is His way of saying, *Look around. Even here, I am caring for you.* Grief can close our eyes to beauty, but when we lift our gaze—even just for a moment—to what God continues to sustain, we remember that the world is still held together by the same hands that hold us. What I love about this verse is that it keeps revealing something new. It calls us to rest in God when life is peaceful and also when life has come undone, to trust Him when we understand the path and when the way ahead feels strange and unknown. The same God who clothes the lilies in splendor carries us through every season.

There were days after my dad died when I could not pray. Days when I had no words and no strength and no clarity. On those days, this verse became a kind of anchor. It reminded me that I did not have to work my way back to God or perform my faith or prove my trust. I could simply be held, the way the lilies are held, without striving or spinning or figuring it all out.

Grief is not a place where we need to be strong. It is a place to be honest, to let our tears fall, and to trust that God is still at work even when we cannot see it. The lilies remind me that even when life feels impossible, God is still caring for what is hidden. He is still tending to what seems forgotten.

And He is still holding us, even now.

In Prayer

Father, Thank You for caring for me the way You care for the lilies. When grief feels heavy and I do not know what to do next, remind me that I do not have to strive to be held by You. Help me rest in Your care, trust what I cannot see, and believe that even here, You are growing something new in me. Amen.

Sit with this

In what ways have you felt the need to "labor and spin" in your grief, trying to fix or understand what has been lost?

How might you begin to rest in God's care, trusting that He is tending to what you cannot see or control?

Grief May Result in Praise

A Verse to Hold

"In all this you greatly rejoice, though now for a little while you may have had to suffer grief in all kinds of trials. These have come so that the proven genuineness of your faith—of greater worth than gold, which perishes even though refined by fire—may result in praise, glory and honor when Jesus Christ is revealed."

1 Peter 1:6–7 (NIV)

Can praise really rise from grief? When your heart is breaking, worship feels far away. Joy feels quiet. Praise feels unfamiliar, like a song you used to know but cannot remember the words to. You wonder if anything good can rise from a heart that feels cracked open.

Yet Peter tells us something that feels both comforting and challenging. He says our trials refine our faith like gold purified by fire. Peter is not saying God causes every trial to refine us. He is saying that when trials come—from living in a fallen world, from others' choices, from circumstances beyond our control—God does not waste them. He uses them to reveal what is genuine. Loss does not weaken faith as much as it shows where it is anchored. And the praise that rises after grief is not shallow. It is honest. It is costly. It is the kind of worship that knows exactly what it costs to trust God again.

There are moments in life that feel like the fire Peter describes. Making the heartbreaking choice to end life support. Facing the end of a marriage. Packing a home filled with memories. Letting go of a dream that shaped your identity. Losing a friendship that can no longer hold who you are becoming. If you are in one of these places today, you know exactly what this fire feels like. These moments feel like they are burning through everything familiar. But it is in these places that faith is tested and shaped. This is where worship becomes something deeper than a song. It becomes surrender. It becomes survival.

So how do we praise God when we are hurting? Most often, it starts small. Sometimes praise is a shaky breath that says, *God, I am still here.* Other times it is a tear during prayer or a quiet *Thank You* that barely forms. Sometimes it is simply opening your Bible when your heart feels numb. Praise in grief is rarely loud. It is usually quiet and unfinished. But it is real.

Praising God in pain does not mean pretending the pain is gone. It means bringing the pain into His presence. It means saying, *God, I do not understand this, but I will keep looking for You.* It says, *This hurts, but You are still good.* It notices small mercies: breath in your lungs, sun through the window, a friend who checks in, the way grief has softened your compassion.

Praise in these moments is not performance. It is formation. It is the fire shaping what is inside you.

And over time—slowly, unevenly, without fanfare—something begins to shift. It does not happen all at once. There are still hard days, still moments when the weight returns. But gradually, you notice that the same circumstances that tried to break you are beginning to reveal strength you did not know you had. Faith grows. Gratitude deepens. God's presence, once hard to feel, becomes familiar again.

You start to realize that even the days you only survived were worship in their own way. That worn faith was still faith. Those days were evidence that your faith, though tested, was still alive, sustained not by your strength, but by His grace.

One day, when you can lift your voice again, it will not be because the grief is gone. It will be because God met you in it. That is what Peter means when he says these trials *"result in praise."* Not polished praise, but true praise. The kind that says, *You have been with me all along.* The God who uses even trials to refine our faith is the same God who stays near through the fire.

If you can believe that, even a little, that small belief is the beginning of praise.

In Prayer

God, You see the ache I carry. You know the nights I have questioned Your goodness and the mornings I have woken up unsure if I could face another day. Still, You stay near. Teach me how to praise You in the middle of what I do not understand. Help me to trust that You are refining my heart, not rejecting it. Let my grief become the place where faith grows deeper, steadier, truer. And when I cannot find the words, hear my silence as worship. In Jesus' name, Amen.

Sit with this

What would it look like for you to offer God praise *in* your current season, not after it ends?

Which parts of your story feel too painful to bring before God, and how might honesty itself become your first act of worship?

Surely Light Will Find Me Here

A Reflection

In the beginning, when grief was still sharp and fresh, I searched for reasons. Why this person? Why now? Why like this? I dug through memories as if closure might be discovered like a clue, as if understanding would somehow quiet the ache.

My father's passing came from cardiac arrest, something sudden and final. We had the medical report. We knew the cause. Still, it changed nothing. The fact was clean. The grief was not. Throughout all his health challenges, his heart was never the concern. It was the part of him we relied on, the part we trusted most. Maybe that is what made it harder to grasp. The part symbolizing his strength was the part that gave out.

One of my closest friends, who works in healthcare, gently told me that nothing could have changed what happened. She explained how cardiac arrest leaves only a brief window to act. By the time my mother found him, that window had closed. Her kind explanation brought a small measure of peace, but the ache remained.

I had wanted the miracle. The testimony. The ending wrapped in light. Instead, there was silence, the kind Mary felt when she said, *Lord, if You had been here.*

What I hold now is the comfort of knowing he left this world in his favorite place, at home, with my mother beside him. Even though that peace carries longing.

Over time, I've learned that faith is not built on answers. Sometimes faith is the courage to keep living without demanding them.

I had to stop asking why and start learning to live with what is. That shift didn't happen all at once. It came slowly, in small moments where I had to choose to keep participating in a world that had broken my heart.

Healing isn't arriving the way I expect. I keep hoping for a moment when I can say I am *better*. Instead, healing is arriving quietly, in ways I almost miss. It shows up in sunlight spilling across the wall, in laughter that doesn't sting, in the taste of something that reminds me I still want to live.

In the beginning, I moved through my days in slow motion: wake, work, sleep, repeat. But somewhere in that fog, light slipped back in and began to guide me. Not bright or obvious, just gentle reminders that something inside me is still alive.

Part of my healing comes from a place people told me to avoid. After the funeral, people said not to visit his grave too much. They said it would keep me stuck. But I need it. There is something about seeing the settled earth now that keeps me connected to him. It feels honest, like the ground itself grieved with me and understands.

I go at random times, sometimes with a purpose and sometimes without one, and I sit, talk, or cry. Those visits have become a kind of conversation I didn't know I needed. When the rest of the world keeps moving, that quiet space lets me stop. I can take my unanswered questions there, along with the memories that make me laugh even as I cry.

As I sit there, I sense that I am not alone. Even though no one physically stands beside me, the Holy Spirit does. I feel the nearness in the stillness, in the breeze moving through the trees, in the peace that meets me after the tears. The Holy Spirit sits with me in that sacred place, not rushing me, simply being present. There is comfort in knowing that God visits the grave too, that His presence doesn't stay behind at the church or the prayer meeting but follows me into the places where my heart still breaks.

As the earth settled, so did I. Seeing the ground become solid again helped me realize that love doesn't go away. It just changes form.

Slowly, almost quietly, light began to thread itself back into ordinary moments, coexisting with the grief.

Once, at the start of football season, I walked into a store filled with Alabama and Auburn gear. If you're from the South, you know what that means. Football is practically a family member. Without thinking, I scanned the racks, looking for something new my dad didn't already have, something I could have given him for Christmas.

Panic hit me, and tears came quickly, catching me off guard. I had to remind myself again that he was gone. I paused for a moment to gather myself and then walked through the area more slowly. That's grief

At one time, I would have left the store in tears. But this time, I stayed. I touched a few sweatshirts and smiled, remembering him shouting at the referees through the TV after a bad play. Then I laughed thinking about the Kick Six game when Alabama lost to Auburn in the literal last second—a cornerback returning a missed field goal 109 yards for the game-winning touchdown in 2013. My dad was so mad that he didn't answer my calls for two days. Even now, that memory makes me laugh. I laughed again remembering when I jokingly poured water over his head to help celebrate an Alabama championship with him. The joy on my dad's face every time Alabama won a championship (even if it's not my team) is something I will always carry

I remember. I breathe. And I keep moving. That's grace and grief coexisting.

It may take me a long time to fully accept my father's death. He has no business being dead. Maybe I never will fully accept it, at least not in the way people expect. But I'm learning that healing isn't about reclaiming what is gone. It's about trusting that the memories that remain are sacred.

Healing grows in unseen places. It grows when I breathe through pain, when I show up for life, when I choose small acts of courage. I may not see it, but I'm healing even through the tears, the doubts, and the long stretch between the past and what comes next.

There will be moments in this journey that undo me: a smell, a song, a holiday. I let the moments come. I cry when I need to. I sit quietly when I must. Then, when I'm ready, I rise again.

This is what I'm learning about living with grief. The loss will live with me, but it won't own my breath. Grief and grace will coexist. The world hasn't ended. It has changed.

One morning, I'll notice the light hits differently. I'll laugh without guilt. I'll make plans for the future. The ache will still be there, but it won't stop me anymore.

Healing is not a task to complete. It's the slow work of living with change and loss. Like light easing through blinds, healing grows quietly.

I'm already healing. The light is returning.

Less Likely to Unravel

A Verse to Hold

"Your eyes have seen my unformed substance; and in Your book were all written the days that were appointed for me, when as yet there was not one of them [even taking shape]."

Psalm 139:16 AMP

When I was growing up, my mom loved to cross-stitch. She would use tiny X-shaped stitches to slowly create a picture, one thread at a time. She kept a basket full of Aida cloth, thread, needles, and patterns. One of my favorites, which I still have, says, *"Life outlined with prayer is less likely to unravel."* I look at it sometimes and think about the patience it took to make it.

Every piece she made was unique. She worked slowly and never rushed. She chose her colors carefully, sometimes adding shades that made no sense until the whole design came together. When she finished, she had the picture framed and sealed so the design could never be changed.

Psalm 139 reminds us that God sees our lives with similar care and attention. Before any of our days began, He already knew each one. He knows what He is doing in us, even when we do not. The bright and dark seasons, the simple and complex parts—all of these threads become part of a story He is faithful to complete.

Grief can feel like unraveling. It can make us feel like we are coming apart, leaving rough edges that refuse to smooth down. It stands out, clear and painful, reminding us of what has been lost. But even here, God's redemptive work continues. He does not waste what brokenness has touched. The painful seasons may not fit the story we hoped for, but God knows how to bring redemption through them. The places that seem unfinished to us are often the places where His presence is strongest. What feels like the end of something good can become the very place where He begins something new.

The threads of your story that include grief are not wasted. They are sacred. These are the moments when faith trembled and tears softened the soil for something new to grow. They do not mean God caused the pain; they show His promise to stay close to the brokenhearted. Looking back, you may see that the hardest days shaped your compassion, deepened your faith, and strengthened your hope. God kept working even when life felt like it was falling apart. The season that once brought pain may one day become the place where His redemptive grace shines brightest.

Some beauty only shows up through the process of healing. It does not shine but has a quiet glow. It is the beauty of endurance, of holding on to God when nothing makes sense, of getting up on hard mornings and choosing trust again. That kind of faith stands out the most.

When God looks at your life, He sees everything at once: the bright seasons, the dark seasons, and the ones still unfolding. Nothing surprises Him. He knows every day before it comes, and He works all things together for His good purpose (Romans 8:28). His restorative work is never rushed or careless. It is full of purpose and love.

So when grief makes you feel unraveled, remember your story is still held together by His hands. Even when life feels fragile, He walks with you through it. God redeems what sin and brokenness have touched, and His heart toward you is always good.

Your story is no less beautiful because it includes pain. In fact, pain often reveals just how deep His grace goes. The contrast between seasons of light and seasons of darkness shows the depth of His faithfulness. Without them, we might never know how steady He truly is.

You may not see it now, and that is okay. And if I am honest, writing this is not easy. My heart still carries threads that feel out of place—the ones I wish God had already tucked in. But I am writing what I know to be true and speaking it over my own life, trusting my heart will catch up. It is an act of surrender, releasing the need for quick fixes and choosing instead to trust that God is still working, even here.

Even when we cannot see how God will redeem our story, we can trust that He is faithful and good. The same God who saw you before you were born still sees you now. The same God who knows every day of your life still holds you close. When He looks at your story, your grief, and your healing, He calls you His beloved. Maybe that is how we learn to stay steady and less likely to unravel—by remembering that even our frayed edges are held by His hands.

In Prayer

God, You are the weaver of my story. You have seen every day of my life before one of them came to be. When I look at the threads that feel out of place or too painful to carry, remind me that they are not wasted in Your hands. Teach me to trust Your design even when I cannot see the full picture. Help me believe that what looks unfinished to me is already complete in Your eyes. Thank You for holding every stitch, every tear, and every moment with care. May my life reflect the beauty of Your faithfulness. Amen.

Sit with this

Where in your life right now do you feel like a "loose thread," something that does not make sense or feels out of place in your story?

How might God be using the darker or more painful threads in your story to reveal His faithfulness and shape your compassion?

This is My Story

A Verse to Hold

"Father, if You are willing, take this cup from me; yet not my will, but Yours be done."

Luke 22:42 (NIV)

How many times have we prayed for our circumstances to change? We could list so many things: relationships, finances, health, timing, and peace. We pray, hope, and wait. There are parts of our story we never imagined. As children, we dreamed of grown-up lives that made sense. The future seemed simple: work hard, love deeply, stay faithful, and things would fall into place. We did not know adulthood would bring tears we could not explain or choices that would break our own hearts. We did not know faith sometimes means holding on when there is no visible reason to.

I think about that often. How none of us saw certain pages of our story coming. We thought some people would stay forever, and some doors would always open. Yet life shows us how fragile our plans are. There is humility in realizing the strongest hopes can bend under reality's weight. Sometimes I wish life were easier. I wish people were kinder, and I wish we were stronger. Not because I expect a life without loss, but because I wish the losses came with a little more warning, maybe even a gentler landing. And when those landings feel rough, it makes us question the formulas we grew up believing. We heard that if we did certain things, we would get certain results. Pray, be kind, love well, and it will circle back to you. Over time, you start to see those rules do not always hold. You can do everything "right" and still end up somewhere you never intended to be. When that happens, it can feel like failure, but it is not. Sometimes it is growth that just is not pretty yet.

God doesn't waste what we've suffered. He redeems the broken parts of our story and can bring meaning even from what was meant to destroy us. Unanswered prayers grow endurance. Silent seasons deepen trust. Delays that once frustrated you begin to reveal themselves as protection rather than punishment.

If I am honest, I have often prayed for God to change my circumstances. Sometimes, He has. Sometimes, He has not. But in every season, He has been changing me—not because the pain was His plan, but because His grace meets me in it. It is not always the answer I want, but it is often the answer I need.

There is this quiet shift that happens when we stop begging for escape and start asking for endurance. It does not mean we stop desiring more. It means we begin to see that His grace is more. That He is still working, still moving, even in what looks like a pause.

Maybe that is what Jesus felt in the garden. He knew what was coming, yet He still asked God for another way. There was no shame in His request. Only honesty and surrender.

If it is possible, take this cup from me. But not my will. Yours.

That moment reminds me that God can handle our honesty. He is not asking us to pretend we are okay. He meets us right in the ache, in the questions, in the uncertainty. Jesus showed us that surrender is not weakness. It is the willingness to trust God's heart, even when the path is painful.

When life feels uncertain, trust means showing up anyway. Not with perfect strength, but with the same trembling honesty Jesus carried into the garden. He prayed through sweat and tears that soaked the ground beneath Him. Trust looks like that sometimes. Doing the next thing with a heart that hurts. Whispering the next prayer with eyes still wet. Believing God sees every drop.

Here is the truth I keep coming back to. This *is* my story, with all its unexpected turns. God didn't script every painful part, but He promises to walk through all of it with me and bring redemption from what was broken. Every part of it—every joy, triumph, heartbreak, delay, and detour—He is faithful to redeem for His purposes. You do not have to understand all of it to live a meaningful, well-lived life.

And this is where gratitude helps us breathe again. It slows you down. It reminds you that there is still beauty, even here. The breath you just took is grace. The sunrise you did not plan to see is mercy. Gratitude does not erase the ache. It softens it enough for hope to slip in. What once felt like loss might one day reveal God's faithfulness in ways you didn't expect. Delays may turn out to be mercy. Gratitude reminds us that every season, even the confusing ones, can still be holy.

So, when your story does not go as planned, remember this. You are not behind. You are not forgotten. You are not being punished. You are simply in a chapter where God's presence matters more than explanations. Whether you are celebrating, grieving, or starting over, keep worshiping in your story. Keep showing up. Your story is not always easy, but God's redemptive work in it is beautiful in ways you do not see yet. He is still writing. He is still redeeming. He is still near.

And even when these pages do not look like you imagined, His grace is enough for this chapter of the story.

In Prayer

God, when life doesn't make sense, help me trust that You are still writing my story. When I want to run or rewrite the ending, remind me that You are with me in every chapter. Give me peace to wait, courage to stay, and eyes to see Your hand in the pages that hurt. Amen.

Sit with this

Think of a part of your story that didn't turn out how you hoped. What did you learn about God's presence or your own strength through it?

The Light That Stays

A Verse to Hold

"If I say, 'Surely the darkness will hide me and the light become night around me,' even the darkness will not be dark to You; the night will shine like the day, for darkness is as light to You."

Psalm 139:11–12 (NIV)

Truth matters deeply in seasons of loss. Because grief alters your relationship with light, not just physical brightness, but the spiritual warmth of God's felt presence. Morning arrives, but the brightness feels washed out. The world keeps humming while every part of you aches. Everything familiar becomes muted, distorted, and heavy.

Psalm 139 tells us something profound about God. It shows us that darkness, the thing we fear and stumble through, is not dark to Him at all. What looks like night to us still shines in His sight. His presence does not shrink when our world collapses. His ability to see us does not dim. We mistakenly think darkness means absence. Scripture teaches that to God, darkness is as light, and it often becomes the very setting where His nearness becomes unmistakable.

Sometimes His ever-present light becomes visible through people who sit in your darkness—a meal on your doorstep, an unexpected message, laughter that surprises you. These small moments are not coincidences. They are glimpses of the light that remains.

I experienced one of those glimpses at a women's worship service at my church. I did not want to go that night. Grief makes even familiar places feel unfamiliar. I stood in my closet thinking it would be easier to stay home and cry. But I sensed God's gentle nudge urging me out the door. My friend Samantha met me there, and with her, I did not have to pretend. When worship started, the room lifted. Hands raised. Voices full. It was the kind of worship that usually pulls me straight in. But I could not move. I stood there with the music swirling around me, unable to sing or reach for God the way I normally would. My heart felt heavy, and I was just trying to survive the moment.

Then our pastor stepped forward between songs. Her voice was soft, the room settled, and she said she felt led to pray for women carrying grief. No one really knew the extent of heartbreak I was enduring, but every word felt strangely specific. She prayed for the woman trying to worship through tears. For the one whose life had shifted overnight. For the one who felt unseen in her pain. Something inside me loosened. Not dramatically. Just a quiet crack where a little light slipped in. It felt like God was touching the part of my grief I could not articulate, reminding me gently of what Psalm 139 promises: the darkness I feel is not dark to Him. He sees me clearly even when I cannot see myself.

Other times you become aware of His light within you—a fragile strength you did not know you had, a quiet prayer whispered through tears, a small will to try again. That strength is not your own resilience. It is God with you. It is evidence that His presence remained steadfast when grief entered the room.

For a long time, I thought light was proof of God's goodness. When life was peaceful and prayers were answered, that was when I believed God was near. Grief taught me something deeper. Scripture says His light does not just shine. It stays. It stays when your heart is breaking. It stays when life does not look recognizable. It stays even when you cannot feel it. The light that stays does not erase pain, but it illuminates the next step. It softens harsh edges. It steadies you when everything else feels shaky. And it reminds you that God's nearness is not fragile.

If you are standing in your own darkness right now, may Psalm 139 be your reminder. You do not need to rush your healing or force yourself into clarity. God has not lost sight of you. Even the places that feel shadowed and unfamiliar are bright to Him.

His presence is the light that stays. His closeness is the hope that carries you. And even now, especially now, He is the One guiding you through the dark into a softer dawn.

In Prayer

God, the world feels dim right now. My heart is tired and my faith feels thin, but I am still here. Help me to feel Your presence, even when I cannot see the light. Teach me that You are not just the God of the sunrise but the God who sits with me through the night. Let Your quiet light stay near, steady, patient, and unshaken. Help me believe that You are still here, and that one day, the light will return. Amen.

Sit with this

Where have you noticed small glimpses of light, even if they seem faint?

How has your understanding of God's presence changed in the dark?

Can't Go Under It

A Reflection

A few weeks after my dad's funeral, I found myself wandering through Target in that dazed, floating way grief makes you move. I didn't need anything. I just needed to be somewhere that wasn't my house, touching things that required nothing from me. Shampoo bottles. Throw pillows. Picture frames I'd never buy.

Then I turned a corner and there it was: a bright blue cover in the children's book section. *We're Going on a Bear Hunt.*

I hadn't thought about that book in years. I loved it when I was a kid. Read it to my nephew when he was little. But standing there in the Target aisle, something pulled me toward it. I picked it up without thinking. Maybe I needed something familiar. Something simple. Something from a time when life didn't hurt quite so much.

I didn't analyze it. I just held the book for a moment, thumbing through the pages, until I landed on those lines I'd sung a hundred times before:

"We can't go over it. We can't go under it. Oh no, we've got to go through it."

I said them under my breath. And that's when it hit me.

Through everything I was going through at this very moment, that simple little chant meant something completely different.

Losing a parent does something strange inside you. It makes you feel small again in ways you can't quite explain. You might be grown, paying bills, making serious decisions, but some part of you becomes a child again, looking for the person who once made the world feel steady. I think about that moment in the garden when I instinctively reached for my phone and called my dad, forgetting, just for a second, that he was already gone. That's what I mean. No matter how adult I am, I still need my dad for so much. He would have been the one I leaned on as I tried to make sense of my broken marriage. He would have been my anchor while everything else was falling apart, the one who reminded me which way was up.

So the story follows a family on an adventure to find a bear, moving through tall grass, thick mud, and a dark forest. Every time they encounter something difficult on their journey, they repeat those same lines: "We've got to go through it!"

I think about that often when it comes to grief because it captures something honest most of us don't want to admit: there's no shortcut through it. No detour around the ache. No map that lets you skip the parts you don't feel strong enough to face.

I tried anyway. I stayed busy, filled my days, convinced myself that being strong meant moving quickly and faith meant smiling through it.

Grief didn't care. It insisted on being felt.

For a stretch of this journey, my tall grass and thick mud showed up as alcohol. I've never been much of a drinker. I didn't touch my first alcoholic drink until I turned 21, and even now I can count on one hand the number of times I've been drunk. I enjoy a glass of wine with dinner, a girl's night wine tasting, or a cocktail that tastes like Kool-Aid, but it would be unusual for me to do much more than this. However, grief has a way of pushing you toward anything that promises to soften the edge. So I reached for alcohol. Not because it tasted good, but because it quieted the ache for a little while. I told myself it helped me get through the nights, even though deep down I knew it wasn't helping at all.

It started with a glass during dinner, something I'd either DoorDashed or barely found the strength to cook. I told myself it was harmless, that since I was such a lightweight it might even help me sleep. After a few weeks, though, something began to shift. One glass turned into two. Two turned into a carefully made girly cocktail to go along with them. Three weeks later, I found myself stopping at the package store after running errands, picking up a new bottle.

The behavior felt foreign and unsettling. And at forty, waking up after that many drinks was neither a small thing nor fun.

One morning after a hangover that made me feel like Fred Sanford faking a heart attack, I could finally see the harm I was causing, and I knew I had to make a different choice. I realized I was trying to outrun something that didn't move. Once the wine wore off, the grief was still there, waiting.

At this time, my husband and I were only separated, still circling the idea of a path forward. So when I realized I needed help, I called him. I told him the truth. I asked him to come take the alcohol out of the house.

He didn't hesitate. He didn't sound disappointed or surprised. He just came.

He moved through the house quietly, like he had done a hundred times before. Opening cabinets. Lifting bottles. Carrying things out without making a show of it. Watching him felt strange, familiar in a way that landed heavy in my chest. For a few minutes, it was easy to forget we were standing in the middle of something broken.

We sat and talked afterward. Nothing dramatic. Just conversation. Small things. Real things. And without meaning to, we fell back into the rhythm of us. The kind that lingers in your body. The kind that reminds you why this person once felt like home. I felt the pull to reach for him, to let myself be comforted in the way I always had. And at the same time, I felt the ache of knowing I could not. That the person who could steady me was also the one who had hurt me. Holding both truths at once was tender and exhausting. Love still present. Trust no longer intact.

It was a gentle moment, but not a simple one. The kind that asks you to sit with the ache instead of trying to resolve it.

And that's the thing about grief: it asks you to sit with a lot of things you'd rather not. The ache of missing someone. The ways you try to numb it. The tender, complicated pull toward someone who hurt you. None of it offers a clean exit.

The book was right. I couldn't go over any of it. I couldn't go under it. I had to walk straight through.

In the story, the family's journey is anything but neat. They stumble, panic, get messy, and run back home breathless. That feels so true to grief. It doesn't move in a straight line. It loops and circles, and some days a single smell or song can undo all the progress you thought you'd made.

I wish I could tell you I had a neat replacement, some specific practice that filled the space where wine and alcohol had lived. But the truth is, I just had to sit with discomfort. I talked about it in therapy. I started walking during the day to quiet some of the anxiety. I took up hot yoga, mostly to learn how to sit in extreme discomfort and not run from it. But mostly, I just had to feel what I'd been trying to avoid. Some nights were harder than others. Some nights I still wanted to reach for something, anything, to soften the edges. But I didn't. Not because I was strong, but because I finally understood that going around wasn't the same as going through.

Going through it had to become a natural rhythm to my life to move forward.

I experienced this on a spontaneous trip to Charleston a few days before Christmas. A few months before that trip, I'd stumbled across a book by an author named Anna Kloots. She's an American writer living in Paris, and her book *My Own Magic* walked through her journey after divorce. I read it during the early days of my own unraveling, and it held me in a season when everything felt uncertain.

I'd been following her on Instagram and saw she was doing a book signing in Charleston around the holidays. Her book had already been out for about a year, but something about the timing felt too intentional to ignore.

Thanksgiving had just undone me. I'd stayed home alone because I couldn't bring myself to sit at a table where I'd expect to see him carving the turkey like he always did. That taught me something: stillness wasn't going to carry me through this season. I needed to move. To get away and grab hold of something that felt like mine—a small act of agency when everything else was out of my control.

So I decided to make the trip. Staying home felt heavier than leaving, and pretending everything was fine felt like too much work. I called it my Blue Christmas vacation.

Blue Christmas isn't an official holiday. It's a name people use for the sad, heavy side of Christmas that doesn't match the glittery commercials. It's the way grievers honor the holidays when absence is part of the celebration. When love is still present, but so is loss. When the world is singing carols and your body remembers who should be here and isn't. Christmas reframed. Sad and beautiful at the same time. A permission slip to feel the ache without pretending it away.

At the event, I was moving through the room, taking in the beauty of it all, when I noticed a tender moment between Anna and her father. It was small and quiet, the kind of moment you only catch when you're paying attention.

And grief hit me hard.

Because when it came to my own writing journey, my dad was always right there. My dad was my biggest cheerleader. When my first book came out, he walked around his job with a plain sheet of printer paper he turned into a makeshift order form. He asked people to write their names, phone numbers, and how many copies they wanted. He collected cash in a white envelope and brought it to me like I didn't have an online order form on my website to ship signed copies. He went old school. Then he made me come home for a visit (I was living in Atlanta at this time), sit down, and sign over forty books for his coworkers. He then hand delivered those books to everyone at his job.

I stood there, watching Anna with her father. It was sweet, and it made my chest ache all at once. Grief looped around me insisting I needed the reminder that the man who always championed my dreams isn't here to walk into these moments with me.

After the book signing was over, I wasn't ready to head back to my hotel just yet. My emotions were still buzzing, and honestly, I just needed something comforting. So I did what any reasonable person would do in December on a solo trip. I googled what restaurant in Charleston had the best desserts.

I'm a sucker for dessert, so when I found a restaurant near the waterfront that had good reviews, I decided to treat myself to a sugary nightcap. They didn't have any available tables, but the hostess told me I could sit at the bar. Perfect. Low stakes, good lighting, no pressure.

I slipped onto a barstool and chatted with the bartender for a bit, telling him why I was in town and that I was stopping in for dessert to end my night. He suggested the crème brûlée—my favorite dessert when the pastry chef nearly burns the top—and without even thinking, I heard a voice in my head say, "I don't eat sweets."

And that's when my dad showed up again, the way grief sneaks in on both sides of the coin. Because if you knew my dad, you know that was his line. He would loudly declare he didn't eat sweets… right before cutting himself the biggest slice of cake at every family gathering. So even though I'd felt that sharp wave of grief earlier at the book party, here I was on the same night, smiling at a memory that felt soft and familiar. One moment bitter, the next moment sweet. Both true, both mine, both carrying me forward in their own way.

And it's in moments like the book signing, or eating crème brûlée at a bar in Charleston, that over time something begins to shift in the journey with grief.

The tall grass that once tangled my steps becomes easier to move through. The mud still sticks, but it doesn't always bury me. The dark forest lightens, and I start noticing signs of life again, a breeze, a birdsong, a soft beam of light. Each time I stumble, I remind myself of the words I once repeated on a different kind of adventure: we've got to go through it. I realize I'm still in the woods, but I'm not lost anymore. That's what healing looks like. Not triumph, but a gentle remembering that life can still hold beauty. I cry and I smile. I miss what I lost, and I cherish what I had. Love stays. It just changes form.

At the end of *We're Going on a Bear Hunt*, the family finally makes it all the way through the grass, the river, the mud, the forest, the snowstorm, and the cave… and they actually find a bear. Naturally, everyone panics. They run for their lives back through every single obstacle they just trudged through. They get home, slam the door, run upstairs, and hide under the covers. Then they announce, with full commitment, that they are never going on a bear hunt again.

I imagine the bear, bless his confused little heart, just stands outside for a moment like, "Well that could've gone better," and wanders off.

The whole thing ends right back where they started. Safe, breathless, a little wiser, and absolutely done with adventure for the day.

Here's where grief is different. The family gets to decide they're done. They made it through once, and now they can close the door and rest. But I don't get to announce I'm finished and have grief follow suit. The tall grass grows back. The mud reappears. The dark forest is still there, and some days I have to walk through it all over again.

The difference is that each time through, I'm a little different. A little softer. A little braver. I know the path better. I know I've survived it before. And slowly, the journey that once felt impossible becomes something I can do again, even when I don't want to.

I keep going. Not because the bear hunt ends, but because I'm learning to walk through it carrying both the weight and the wisdom.

That's why the book sits on my shelf now, a children's story that became something else. A reminder that going through is the only way. That bravery is not loud or fearless, but willing. Willing to take the next step even when your legs are tired and your heart remembers how hard the last stretch was.

Some days, all I can do is name where I am. Tall grass again. Mud again. The edge of the forest. And that has to be enough. Grief does not ask us to conquer it, only to keep showing up. To keep choosing movement over numbness. To trust that rest is not gone, just postponed.

I am learning that courage looks like walking forward with memory and hope sharing the same body. Like letting joy return in pieces. Like believing that even if the path loops back on itself, I am not starting from nothing. I am carrying evidence now.

And when I get tired, I trust the same God who walks with me through the water will also teach me how to sit beside it again. Not rushing. Not performing healing. Just resting. Breathing. Alive.

If you are somewhere on the path too, I hope you know this. You are not failing because it feels hard again. You are not weak because the terrain looks familiar. You are still moving. And that counts. Sometimes it counts more than anything else.

More Beautiful Than the Original

A Verse to Hold

"He has made everything beautiful in its time."

Ecclesiastes 3:11 NIV

Kintsugi is a Japanese art that restores broken pottery using lacquer mixed with gold, silver, or platinum. The practice is rooted in the belief that breakage and repair are part of an object's history—not something to disguise, but something to illuminate. When you look at a restored piece, what makes it breathtaking is that the cracks are not hidden. They are honored. The repair becomes part of the story, a visible reminder of what was broken and made whole again.

I return to this image often because it mirrors how God works in our lives. The world expects perfection. It tells us to tuck away our pain and act as if nothing ever shattered. But the Gospel moves differently. Jesus bore scars even after resurrection (John 20:27). God reveals His beauty through the very places we would rather hide.

When a heart breaks, God does not discard it. He does not tell you to sweep the pieces away and start over. He gathers every fragment with care and begins the slow, patient work of restoration. Ecclesiastes 3 reminds us that there is a time for everything: a time to break down and a time to build up, a time to weep and a time to laugh, a time to lose and a time to be made new. These words help us release the pressure to understand every season. They remind us that even in the breaking, God is already shaping something beautiful in His time.

Grief can break us wide open. It arrives without warning and fractures what once felt steady. Suddenly you are holding pieces of your own heart, unsure how to fit any of them back together. Your confidence slips. Your laughter fades. Everything familiar feels far away. And even then, God stays close. He does not scold you for your tears or rush your process.

But here is the thing about healing in grief: the pieces must be gathered before they can be mended. Restoration takes time, and every part of that process is sacred.

With time, grace begins to fill the cracks. Slowly, light returns. What once hurt the most begins to shine with a beauty that only brokenness can teach you to see. This is how grace works. It does not erase pain. It transforms it. Just as the golden lacquer strengthens broken pottery, God's grace strengthens the tender places in us. What once seemed ruined becomes a sign of His faithfulness.

Looking back over my life, I see those golden lines forming in places I once tried to hide. The end of my marriage is one of them. There were days when I felt like scattered pieces, unsure if anything good could come from what fell apart. I wondered if this fracture made me less whole, less wanted, less worthy of love. But that was a lie grief whispered, not the truth God's promises proclaim. My worth had never been tied to my circumstances. It was rooted in His unchanging love for me.

I thought I needed to heal quietly and quickly so no one would see what had cracked. But God met me right there. He did not ask me to deny what happened or expect me to put the pieces back together with my own hands. He gathered them gently and began the slow work that healing requires. Some days the progress was so subtle I could not see it. Other days I felt my breath deepen, as if hope was finding its way back. Little by little, His grace filled the places that hurt. Little by little, the cracks began to shine.

Grief changes how you see the world. It slows you down and helps you notice small mercies again: warm morning light, unexpected kindness, quiet space to breathe. Wholeness starts to look different too. You realize it is not about going back to who you were. It is about allowing God to reshape you. True wholeness is not perfection. It is the assurance that even in the cracks, God's grace has never left you.

A finished kintsugi piece is not fragile. The gold lacquer makes it stronger than before. In the same way, God's healing does not make you weaker. It deepens compassion. It expands your capacity for love. It anchors you in hope. Every scar and fracture, every place that once hurt, can now hold light. The gold lines in your story do not show defeat. They show grace. They say, *I walked through brokenness, but I did not stay there.* They whisper, *God was faithful, even here.*

Your story does not end with what was broken. It continues with what God is restoring. If grief has changed you, surrender to how God is shaping you with purpose through it. Let Him soften you where you once felt hardened and strengthen you where you once felt fragile. When others look at your life, they will not see the end of your story. They will see God's grace at work in the restoration, shining through the cracks like gold.

In Prayer

Thank You for taking the broken pieces of my life and filling them with Your gold of grace and mercy. When I am tempted to hide my cracks, remind me that they are proof of Your healing hand. Help me to trust the process, to sit with You in the waiting, and to believe that You are making something beautiful out of what was once broken. Amen.

Sit with this

What parts of your story still feel too broken to be seen, and how might God be inviting you to trust Him with those pieces?

In what ways can you begin to see the "gold" in your healing, the evidence of God's grace where pain once lived?

When the Foundation Looks Too Small

A Verse to Hold

"The glory of this present house will be greater than the glory of the former house," says the Lord Almighty.

Haggai 2:9

Starting over can feel like walking into a room where nothing belongs to you. You look around and think, *None of this matches what I imagined for my life.* The future you expected disappears, and the new beginning does not feel exciting.

When your world changes, part of you goes silent. You stop dreaming for a while because disappointment still stings. You start questioning everything, including yourself. *Was I naïve? Was I too hopeful? Did I miss something God was trying to warn me about?* And then the worst one: *What if my best days already happened?* That question can sit heavily on your chest.

Haggai spoke to people who felt the same way. They had lost the temple that held all their memories of God's glory. Looking at the new foundation, it seemed small and unimpressive compared to what they remembered. They wondered if God's presence would ever feel as real as before.

God did not blame them for grieving what they lost. He validated their sorrow. But He told them not to judge the future by the past—not because the past did not matter, but because He had new promises to fulfill. He promised that what is coming will be even greater than what was lost. Not the same. Not a copy. *Greater.*

It is hard to believe that when everything you hoped for has fallen apart. When the place you called home feels empty. When you wake up alone and memories linger everywhere. When love changes, people leave, jobs end, and dreams break. Rebuilding does not feel special. It just feels like getting by. I used to think starting over meant celebrations and excitement. But most of the time, it comes with tears and hard conversations. Sometimes God's provision looks like hard work, and sometimes the blessing is simply that you are still standing.

When you are rebuilding, it is easy to believe that what you had before was the best it will ever be. You might think happiness is gone for good. But that is not true. God is not just about the past. He is about what is still possible. He does not just reuse what is left; He creates new beauty and hope from what is broken.

God will grow things in this new season that you could not have imagined before, not because the loss was necessary, but because His faithfulness meets you wherever you are. You are finding strength that only comes from rebuilding, even when it is hard. Wisdom is forming through your tears, and courage is growing just because you keep going.

Haggai's people mourned the past while God promised them a future. I have done the same, looking back at what used to be. But God keeps reminding me, *Keep going. I am not finished. What I am building now has a glory you cannot see yet.*

The healing is slow. Sometimes you feel like you are taking two steps forward and two steps back. Sometimes you do not even want to take any steps. But slowly, you start to notice the little signs that you are becoming someone new. You laugh a little louder again. You sleep a little better. You start dreaming again without feeling guilty. You make plans that do not include the person or the future that ended. It feels scary, but it is also holy.

You can honor the past while moving forward. You can grieve what you lost and still trust that the new will feel like home someday. Haggai 2:9 is that quiet but audacious promise that God is not done showing up just because things look smaller, slower, or stripped down. The latter glory will be greater than the former—not louder, not flashier, but deeper. Less spectacle, more substance. What feels like a rebuild season is not a downgrade. It is a refinement. God is not trying to recreate what was. He is doing something truer, something steadier, something that can actually hold peace this time.

This new version of your life is part of that promise: even when the past feels irreplaceable, what is ahead can be greater, not because what you lost was inadequate, but because His redemptive power is that strong. Let that hope anchor you as you rebuild.

In Prayer

God, remind me that the story is not finished and the loss is not the end of goodness in my life. Take the places that feel empty and fill them with Your presence. Breathe hope into the corners where fear tries to settle. Thank You that what is ahead can be greater than what is behind. Help me believe that I am still becoming everything You imagined when You created me. Amen.

Sit with this

When you think about your future, what fears speak the loudest and what truths could speak louder?

What small signs show you that God is rebuilding your life even if the progress feels slow.

What would it look like to believe that God has greater ahead for you, not in theory but in reality.

The God in Your Corner

A Verse to Hold

We are pressed on every side but not crushed. Perplexed but not in despair. Persecuted but not abandoned. Struck down but not destroyed.

2 Corinthians 4:8-9

Grief can feel like an uninvited roommate. It shows up, takes what you value, and acts as if you are the one intruding. Losing someone or something important can make it seem like the ground beneath you has vanished. You keep standing, though you are not sure how. You keep breathing, and each deep breath surprises you.

Some days, the ache feels louder than hope. You wonder if you will ever stop feeling this tired. You wonder if you will ever stop checking your phone for a text that is not coming. You wonder if you will ever stop replaying the last normal moment before everything changed.

That is where Paul meets us. He was not at ease when he wrote these words. He was facing real hardship. Even as he described how hard life can be, he also spoke about God's truth. *Pressed but not crushed. Perplexed but not in despair. Persecuted but not abandoned. Struck down but not destroyed.* There is a pattern:

every painful reality is met by God's presence and protection. We can be honest about our pain without worrying that honesty undermines our faith.

Sometimes I believed that to show I trusted God, I had to be strong and put together. I tried to hold back my tears, push through the hardest days, keep my prayers neat even when my heart was hurting. But God does not need me to pretend. He meets me in my mess. He sits with me when I am confused. He does not turn away when I say, *God, this still hurts.*

And it does still hurt. Even after months or years have passed. Even after you have tried everything to heal. Even when you find yourself laughing again. Grief quietly lingers in the background. It appears at the grocery store, in a song, or when you catch a familiar scent. It does not matter if you are doing your best. Grief just comes. But here is what I am learning: I do not have to hate grief. It reminds me that what I lost mattered. It means love was real and the connection was deep. I would rather feel the ache of something that shaped me than feel nothing at all. Love leaves a mark, and grief is often proof of the imprint.

The important thing is this: grief does not get to tell the whole story. God stays. God holds. God gives strength. God mends what is broken, little by little. He does not wait for you to feel brave. He walks with you when you are struggling.

I used to think healing meant the tears would eventually stop. Now I know healing often looks like tears and hope sharing the same room. There are days I feel pressed. There are nights I feel perplexed. There are moments I feel struck down. But somehow, I wake up again. Somehow, I show up again. Somehow, there is a flicker of strength that I cannot explain. That flicker is God—His grace sustaining what I cannot sustain myself.

Paul did not ignore the struggle. He named it and said it would not win. He recognized how hard life can be, but he made sure we know we will not be defeated. There is a hand to catch us when we fall. There is a presence every long night. There is a love that never gives up on you.

So if today you feel like grief has you backed into a corner, take a breath. The fact that you are still here is your sign. Strength is still running through you, even if it feels thin. Hope is still breathing, even if quietly. God is still holding you, even when you are too tired to hold on to Him. You are allowed to be human, hurting, and hopeful all at once.

Some days you will carry grief lightly. Some days it will weigh you down. But every day, God carries both of you.

You are not crushed. You are not abandoned. You are not destroyed. You are held.

In Prayer

God, I do not always feel strong. Some days I feel tangled in sadness and tired from the weight of everything I miss. Thank You that my weakness does not push You away. Thank You that You stay when my world feels unsteady. Hold me close when the tears come. Lift me when I feel pressed down. Remind me that nothing can separate me from Your presence. I am not crushed. I am not abandoned. I am Yours, and You are here. Amen.

Sit with this

What are the small ways you can see God sustaining you, even on hard days?

Which word from Paul's list do you feel the most right now: pressed, perplexed, persecuted, or struck down? How can you invite God into that specific place today?

His Peace, Not the World's

A Verse to Hold

"Peace I leave with you. My peace I give you. I do not give to you as the world gives. Do not let your hearts be troubled and do not be afraid."

John 14:27 (NIV)

Let us be honest. When someone tells you to have peace while your whole life has flipped upside down, you want to look at them like, *With what money. With what energy. From where.* I used to think peace was this shiny thing that only showed up when everything was going well, like a reward for people who have never cried in the shower.

Then loss came. Then anxiety showed up and unpacked its bags. The kind of peace I thought I knew washed away.

So when Jesus says, *"I am leaving you peace,"* I want to ask Him, *What kind? Because the kind I used to have does not fit here anymore.*

Jesus spoke these words when His friends were starting to panic. He had just told them He was going away. Everything they depended on suddenly felt shaky. Their stomachs were probably tight. Their breathing was probably shallow. They had no idea what was coming. They just knew something painful was on its way. Which means Jesus did not wait for things to get better to give them peace. He handed it over right in the middle of everything falling apart.

That comforts me more than I can explain.

Because grief comes with anxiety. It is like your heart does not trust the world anymore. A phone call can feel like a threat. A memory can feel like a trap. Your chest can tighten over the simplest things. Some days you wake up and your first thought is, *I do not know how to do this without them.* Then you feel your heartbeat racing like it wants to run ahead of you.

That is why I want you to hear this gently. Peace looks different now. And that does not mean you lost it. It means God is giving you a new kind.

Peace now might be the way you find enough breath to get your shoes on. Peace now might be remembering to eat even when you barely feel hungry. Peace now might be sitting in the car until you feel steady enough to walk inside. Peace now might be letting the tears fall instead of fighting them. Sometimes peace looks like the next tiny step.

Pay attention to the moments when you think, "I should be falling apart more than this," but you are not. Those moments matter. They are not strength you magically found. They are evidence. Someone is holding you together.

Jesus says, *"Not as the world gives."* The world gives peace like a transaction. If you check all the boxes, then you get to feel okay. God gives peace like someone pulling you close so you do not collapse under the weight of it all.

The peace He gives does not say, *It is fine.* It says, *I am right here.*

And maybe that is what peace looks like now. It looks like God sitting with you while your heart aches. It looks like Him placing one hand over your panic and saying, "Breathe." It looks like someone steady beside you in the quiet so you are not alone. It looks like making it through a day you were convinced might break you.

Peace might not feel like calm yet. It might feel like barely getting through. But barely getting through still counts.

But peace that starts small does not stay small. God tends it the way He tends everything—patiently, faithfully, in ways you do not notice until you look back and realize you are standing steadier than you were. The barely-getting-through days become the foundation for something deeper.

I do not know when the light will come back. I do not know when laughter feels natural again. But I do know this: if Jesus promised peace before the worst night of His friends' lives, then He is not waiting for everything to be perfect to give it to you.

He knows you are grieving. He knows you are anxious. He knows you do not trust the ground under your feet. And He is not frustrated by that. He is not waiting for you to get over it. He is staying right here. Right now. In this moment.

The peace He gives does not erase the storm. It reminds you that you are not facing it alone. His presence is the peace.

So if you are wondering where peace is, maybe it is this. It is the breath you just took. It is the tension in your shoulders slowly dropping. It is the tiny bit of hope you cannot explain. It is the fact that you showed up for today.

Maybe peace never needed to be shiny. Maybe presence was the point all along. God is staying with you. And peace is staying too. Even if it feels small. Even if it feels quiet. Even if it feels like trembling.

You are not doing this without Him.

In Prayer

Jesus, I do not feel calm, but I want to trust that Your peace is here anyway. Stay close. Help my breath slow. Help my heart feel held. Thank You for not leaving me in the middle of everything that hurts. Teach me to notice the quiet ways You give me peace, even when my world feels loud with fear. Amen.

Sit with this

How can you give yourself permission to let peace be small while your heart is still healing?

When anxiety rises, what simple phrase or prayer helps you remember you are not facing this moment alone?

The God Who Stays

It's Saturday, November 15, 2025. It has been 523 days since I heard my dad's voice. We have made it through all the grief firsts, barely breathing, but we made it. His birthday. Our birthdays. My parents' forty-first wedding anniversary. Blue Christmas and the gray holidays that followed. Mom has started making small changes in the house. His side of the closet cleared. A picture taken down. Things that feel wrong and necessary at the same time. The dirt at his grave has settled now, but 523 days still feels like day one.

Grief has a strange way of collapsing time. Loss stacks on loss until you cannot tell where one ends and the other begins.

At this point in the journey, the best word I have for my grief is untethered.

I keep thinking about those paper doll chains we made in school. You folded the paper, cut out a little person, then unfolded it and suddenly there were four or five figures, all holding hands. My paper doll chain was my family: my mom, dad, my two sisters, and me. Our original five. Bigger now because of marriage and kids, but still anchored in that first shape.

When I picture my grief, I see myself standing between my parents in that chain. Somewhere along the way, someone cut the place where my dad and I were holding hands. I am still holding my mom's hand, but the other side of me is loose. One arm reaching for something that is no longer there. My balance off. My body unsure of where to settle.

The instinct is to reach for my mother. To grip tighter. To ask her to steady me. But parents give us different things, and she is carrying her own grief. Some days, reaching for her would ask more than she has to give. And even when she can hold on, she cannot fill the space my father left.

So I stand here, connected on one side and cut free on the other, learning how to stay upright without one of the hands that once held me steady. That is what grief feels like to me. Not loud. Not dramatic. Just a quiet, constant untethering.

But 523 days is long enough to lose more than one hand from the chain.

I am no longer married.

No one gets married imagining an ending. No one stands at an altar thinking, We will try this for a while and see how it goes. We walk toward each other believing in forever, believing that love will be a shelter. I loved my husband. I loved being married. I loved being a wife. I loved the small rituals, the shared language, the sense of belonging to someone and being chosen back. But somewhere along the way, love stopped being safe. The covenant was broken, not in one dramatic moment, but in a series of fractures that could not be sealed again. What was meant to be a covering became a wound. And staying no longer honored God, myself, or the truth.

I say the words plainly now, without theatrics, without apology. Not because it was easy, wanted, or clean, but because it was true.

523 days without my father's voice. A marriage ending. Compound grief is what they call it. And here I was on a Saturday morning, needing somewhere to put it all.

I went to Saturday morning prayer for the first time at a church that has taken its sweet time to feel like home. For a while, it wasn't neutral ground. It held the echo of a season when my husband and I sat side by side, hands lifted, believing we were building something that would last. On Sundays I came and went quietly. I did not rush to join. I had only ever been a "we" there, and suddenly it was only me walking through the doors. It took time to believe this place could hold me in a different way. Time to trust that what had once been shared could become a place for me. Time to let God meet me not as part of a pair, but as myself.

I went in and spoke to a few people I had gotten to know and hugged my friend who sang on the worship team. I sat as close to the stage as I could get, wanting to be as close to worship as possible. The music settled into the room, steady and unhurried. The beautiful thing about Saturday morning prayer at any church is that it's early, early enough that it's never crowded. There is space to move, space to breathe, space to let yourself disappear for a moment without being noticed.

Midway through worship, we moved into collective prayer. This is when I pull out my notebook. I don't usually pray out loud in these settings. I am a writer, and words come to me first on the page. Writing is how I listen. It's how I pay attention. It's how I stay present when my thoughts threaten to scatter. So I write prayers instead. I let them form slowly, honestly, without the pressure of being heard.

Somewhere in the middle of it, I felt hands rest on my shoulders. Gentle. Grounding. A woman I had never seen before stood behind me. She didn't introduce herself. She didn't ask permission. She didn't explain. She just stayed.

She prayed quietly, without performance, not rushed. Her voice was steady enough to make me stop writing. The words landed one by one, too precise to be accidental. She prayed over my heavy heart. Over the obedience I had been trying to walk in, even when it cost me more than I expected. Over new life, spoken softly, like something fragile and real.

She could not have known any of that on her own. I did not know her. And standing there, with her hands still on my shoulders, I felt seen in a way that did not require me to explain myself. It was as if God had leaned in close enough to whisper, *I know exactly where you are.*

A little later, a woman I only vaguely knew from the prayer team came over and gently interrupted my writing. She didn't rush me. She waited until I looked up, then asked if I was in a place to talk. Her voice was calm, careful, like she knew she was stepping onto holy ground. She told me she felt prompted to check in and asked what I had been praying about.

I shared a little. Not everything. Just enough. I told her about my father's death. About the divorce. The words came out quieter than I expected, like they had learned to lower themselves over time.

She listened without trying to fix anything. Without hurrying me along. She told me she recognized parts of my story because she had lived pieces of it herself. There was no comparison, no advice dressed up as wisdom. Just recognition.

Before she left, she encouraged me to stay open. To trust God again in the places that feel the most fragile, especially when it comes to love. Not with pressure. Not with promises. Just with the kind of hope that understands how easily a heart can bruise.

The truth is, I didn't want to be at prayer that morning. I had joked with God the night before that I wasn't setting an alarm. I needed rest more than revelation. I needed quiet more than another moment that might ask something of me. Still, I woke up at seven anyway, two hours before prayer even started, my body alert before my courage caught up.

That moment—hands on my shoulders, words I didn't have to speak aloud—pulled me back to the night I stood in the hospital lobby with Uncle Ken, fluorescent lights buzzing overhead, asking the only question I had left. *What do we do now?* I didn't know then. I was standing at the edge of something I could not yet name, let alone navigate.

Standing in worship that morning, I realized how far I've come since that night. And how much I am still learning.

As I write these final pages, I keep thinking about all the things I thought I knew about grief before I lived it. I thought it would be linear. I thought faith would make it "easier." I thought healing meant going back to who I was before. I was wrong about almost all of it.

I never set out to be fluent in grief. It is still something of a mystery to me. Even as these pages come together, I am stumbling my way through healing, learning what it means in real time. I do not have all the answers, and I am finally at peace with that. Maybe we were never meant to master grief. Maybe we were only meant to move through it with honesty, tenderness, and whatever light we can find along the way.

My father got sick just a month before my 2022 wedding. None of us knew if he would even make it to the ceremony. By grace, he did, and we had him for a few more years. My marriage brought me back home to Alabama, and while that marriage did not last, it did something I did not know I needed. It gave me time.

I am not grateful for the pain I walked through in that relationship, and I do not pretend that grieving a marriage and a father at the same time was anything short of devastating. But I can acknowledge this: being here gave me precious time with my dad, time I would not have had if life had gone a different way.

It might take a while, but I know one day I will look back and see that the twists I never would have chosen somehow placed me exactly where I needed to be. Where I could be present for the time we had left, even if I don't fully understand everything else that transpired in the journey.

As my dad got sicker, we settled into a routine we never wanted but had to figure out. We listened for his cough, the soft shuffle of his feet, and could tell how he was feeling by the sounds he made around the house. Even during weeks when we were in the hospital more than at home, those familiar noises anchored us.

When they stopped, the silence felt unbearable. It was like the house forgot how to breathe.

In this season, disappointment nearly broke my faith. Not in a single dramatic moment, but in the slow accumulation: the unanswered prayers, the losses piling up, the silence that met every *Why?* I whispered.

I think about the crowd that followed Jesus until His teaching felt too hard to accept and how quickly they walked away. It would have been simpler to do the same, to turn grief into distance, to let heartbreak harden me. Some days I wanted to. Some days I almost did.

But losing my father and my marriage so close together solidified something in me. Faith is not understanding or the absence of doubt. It's choosing to follow Him anyway. Staying even while you whisper, *"Lord, where else would I go?"*

Recently, the Northern Lights have wandered farther south than usual, spilling across skies that almost never hold that kind of beauty. Strong solar storms can pull the aurora down from the poles, giving everyday neighborhoods a rare glimpse of color. For a few fleeting hours, the sky feels adventurous, reaching toward the people below, painting wonder where it is least expected.

One night last year, I was doing a late-night doom scroll when a neighbor posted in our neighborhood Facebook group. She told everyone to step outside and look up, and she attached a photo of the sky. I grabbed my phone and ran out the door, my heart already racing. I had read you could sometimes catch the lights more clearly through a camera, so I pointed my phone toward the sky and walked down the street in the direction she mentioned, half-believing and half-doubting I'd see anything at all.

And there it was. Faint, but real. Quiet ribbons of color stretching across the night: soft greens, blues, and hints of rose that seemed impossible this far south. I stood there with my neck craned back, watching the colors pulse and fade, reappear and shift—like they were breathing. The kind of thing you'd normally have to chase to the Arctic Circle, and here it was, hanging over my suburban street.

If I weren't a woman of faith, I might have stood there amazed and left it at that. Chalked it up to solar storms and lucky timing. But I couldn't help but think: if beauty this rare can show up in a place it doesn't belong, then maybe God can do the same for me.

Maybe God doesn't care about geography or timing, or the rules I've made up about where grace is allowed to show up. Maybe holiness can happen anywhere—even here, in this messy, sideways place I didn't expect to be. If beauty this rare can show up in unexpected skies, then so can I. Even now. Even in a life that feels too far south for faith or joy to bloom. I don't have to wait for the "right" latitude to believe I belong and can make it through.

The light ribbons moved like whispers, like something sacred showing itself just long enough to remind me there's still so much I have yet to discover about life beyond this season.

I have always believed that when you pay attention to nature, it becomes almost impossible not to believe that God is the creator of the universe, the maker of heaven and earth. So I stood there in the cool night, head lifted to the sky, tears I didn't know were coming blurring the colors above me. God keeps finding new ways to remind me that He shows up. In unexpected places. In unexpected ways. Always at the moment I need it most.

And in that moment, like so many others over the past 523 days, I felt God there, as close as the night air on my skin, and I hadn't done a thing to earn it. I didn't have to plan it, deserve it, or make sense of it. It was enough that I noticed.

The breeze on my face, the quiet sway of the trees, the stars spilling light across the sky—all of it whispered that even when I'm lost, even when I doubt, even when I think I've wandered too far, I am never beyond His reach.

Grief still lives in my body, settling in the spaces between breaths, showing up when I least expect it and refusing to be hurried. Some nights the ache is louder than the stars, and some days the silence feels endless. But even then, even here, I am held. I only have to be still enough to feel it, look up, and notice the light never left.

Final Prayer

God blesses those who mourn, for they will be comforted.

Matthew 5:4 ESV

May you know that your grief is not a detour from God's blessing. May you stop apologizing for how long it takes to heal. May you trust that God is not waiting for you to be finished mourning before drawing near. May comfort find you in ordinary moments. In quiet mornings, in deep breaths, in the simple fact that you are still here.

May you sense God sitting with you, unhurried, unbothered by your tears.

And when the light comes, may it not overwhelm you or demand anything from you.

May it arrive gently.

May it stay.

Amen

www.ingramcontent.com/pod-product-compliance
Lightning Source LLC
LaVergne TN
LVHW020509100826
845148LV00003B/731